ON BECOMING
RESTORED

ON BECOMING RESTORED

A Journey to Wholeness and
Understanding the Seasons of Life

KEMI SOGUNLE

Published by Kemi Sogunle
Copyright ©2014 Kemi Sogunle

All rights reserved. No part of this book may be reproduced, scanned or distributed in any printed or electronic form without permission. Please do not participate in or encourage piracy of copyrighted materials in violation of the author's rights. Purchase only authorized editions.

ISBN: 978-0-9909721-6-7 (Print)
ISBN: 978-0-9909721-7-4 (eBook)

DEDICATION

This book is dedicated to my love, my life and my miracle, Tobi. Giving birth to you has been one of the best things (if not the best) I have done in my life. Thank you for always speaking love to me when I need it most. I pray you find the wisdom to live a purposeful life, just as I continue to drop my nuggets of wisdom into your life daily. You are indeed a shoulder to lean on. Thank you for making me the best Mom ever. I love you always!

ACKNOWLEDGEMENTS

I could not have written this book without the grace and love of God that keeps me going on a daily basis. I give Him all the glory for keeping me alive to this very day. Without Him, I am nothing, nothing at all. I have learned to tune in to hear Him speak to me more than ever before.

To the God who keeps me safe through each day, who continually reminds me that my sole source of everything is Him, who has shown up in my life and journey; I am forever indebted to my Heavenly Father, my all in all. To Him be the glory!

To everyone I have met through life's journey that continues to encourage me, thank you. To everyone reading this book, I pray that your life will be transformed and that you will come to embrace the truth, knowing that the life you deserve already exists, but you have to connect with it in order to truly live.

To all those who taught and continue to teach me directly or indirectly what life is all about and contributed to my journey in any shape or form, I say a big thank you. It all led me to who I am today and helped me connect with the real me (my true essence) as well as the God's purpose for my life: I am grateful.

To my family, I thank you for letting me realize during my most difficult times that it is not always family that I need, but God. Connecting to God, not man, led me to my purpose and gave me the opportunity to learn to love myself irrespective of what life brings. That is what life is all about: Purpose.

To my son: You are everything to me. You are the best gift God ever gave me. Thank you for all the encouraging words that kept me going in the most difficult times. Thank you for always being generous to me and understanding the seasons we live in. I pray that God continues to guide and order your steps according to His will for your life. May His will alone be done in your life. I love you dearly, and more than you can imagine. Thank you for everything!

PREFACE

There are four seasons in life, just as there are four seasons to every year: Spring, summer, fall, and winter. Recognizing the season, you are in, based on where you are in your journey, how connected you are to God (the source of life) and knowing who you are, can result in either an amazing lifestyle or an existence of pain. Realizing that life cannot be lived without The One who created us, but believing and allowing Him to guide and lead us, can help us to understand the seasons of life. Knowing the various elements of each season can bring about a life of love, peace, joy, and abundance when we are grounded and our roots are deep within the foundation of God's amazing love. The four seasons of life are a light along the pathway of your journey to wholeness.

You will experience the season when things start to bloom in your life. There will be the scotching times when you hit the rock bottom and find yourself deep into the roughs. There will come a time when things seem to dry up. This is your wilderness season. At other times, you will experience the separation anxiety season where you will struggle to dissociate yourself from everything that holds you back from becoming a higher level of yourself.

I invite you to take this ride with me and explore the four seasons of life while allowing love to restore you and reset your buttons so that you can begin to live and not just exist from this moment on. If you allow life to teach you the lessons needed to master the course of your journey, you will become the master of your own life (rather than allowing life to master you).

"Your darkest moments will bring your brightest light!"

CONTENTS

INTRODUCTION		1
CHAPTER 1	Growing Up	3
CHAPTER 2	The Polygamy Syndrome	15
CHAPTER 3	High School Days	23
CHAPTER 4	College Days	31
CHAPTER 5	The Quest for Love	41
CHAPTER 6	The Workforce	51
CHAPTER 7	The Journey Continues	59
CHAPTER 8	More Challenges	67
CHAPTER 9	Facing the Odds	75
CHAPTER 10	The Marriage	79
CHAPTER 11	Purpose is Greater Than Life	89
CHAPTER 12	The Separation Anxiety Phase	95
CHAPTER 13	Dead but Alive?	107
CHAPTER 14	The Commitment	115
CHAPTER 15	The Commitment Process	127
CHAPTER 16	The Life Lessons	133
CHAPTER 17	What Lies Ahead	147
BONUS CHAPTER 1	Quotes on Life and Relationship	159
BONUS CHAPTER 2	Daily Affirmations	173
BONUS CHAPTER 3	Thoughts on Life and Relationships	177
ABOUT THE AUTHOR		183

INTRODUCTION

Where do I begin? This journey called *life* has taught me a lot including some things about relationships—the foundation of everything we do. The good ones, the bad ones and the not so good—or bad—ones. Remember that there is no perfect relationship.

I have lived on this Earth for almost fifty years but all the experiences and knowledge I have gained, make it seem as if I have been here longer.

Growing up as a child, I was naïve and a bit sheltered, but I was allowed to explore (to some extent)—thanks to my grandfather, who allowed us to have parties and to let loose while learning to relax and be ourselves. We had everything at our reach: Maids and chauffeurs were there to assist, and this meant we did not have to worry about a lot of things. The opportunity for my brothers and uncles to hold parties exposed me to what life is like for a boy or man as opposed to life for a woman.

However, the separation of my parents left me broken. It tore me apart on the inside, yet I still managed to put a smile on my face and let everyone think I was doing well. This separation was the beginning of my brokenness. This was what led me to draw back into my shell and create a world of hurt and pain in my mind. I saw my parents' broken relationship as part of my problem without realizing that it was their journey, not mine. All I needed to do was to learn from their experience and not repeat their patterns. However, I chose to hold on to the bad memories of their separation while thinking I had contributed to it. Hence, I awakened myself to the life and world of hurt and pain.

Each day opens a new line, a new beginning and a new chapter, but without connecting to God, you may never connect to the scripts He has mapped out for you. I never did earlier on in life but as I continue to grow and find myself, I am learning to rely completely on God. The Holy Spirit cautions me on when to speak and when to listen for clarity. Learning to do this frequently helps me to become who God created me to be, rather than allow the world (society, culture, and tradition) to condition or program my life outside of what my Creator destined it to be.

As you read this memoir and relate to it, may this journey of mine lead you to healing, forgiveness, and letting go of memories that no longer serve you. I share with you some experiences that may help you along your journey. I pray and hope that I can help you connect to your God-given purpose and live truthfully before the final bell of life rings.

CHAPTER 1
Growing Up

I was born into the Sogunle family. A family of wealth and knowledge. It was nothing I planned, but what God deemed. It was the path set before me as a ground for learning about God's purpose for my life. I had no idea what life was about. Being privileged made me a novice at certain things.

I remember going on weekend parties and sleepovers with my parents at their friends' homes. Other times, it was family weekend parties or spending time at my grandparents' home. We had chauffeurs who picked us up from school and dropped us off at my grandparents'. It was the only life I knew. This naive little girl back then had no idea of challenges life would bring.

We were never felt that anything was missing. There were housemaids, chefs, chauffeurs, cleaners, even someone to iron our clothes (the washer man). We hung out with a "class" and that was all the exposure we got. It was all about who you know. My dad was fond of asking any friend who visited us about their parents and what they did for a living. I guess this was his way of exploring the family's background. We were not too exposed to the less wealthy side of life even though we lived around those who did (i.e., those who worked for the family).

I attended a private elementary school in Lagos, where we lived. We wore uniforms; we had handkerchiefs that had to be neatly pinned to our uniforms and white socks to match, plus ribbons in our hair. I recall starting class in elementary school and shielding myself due to my shyness. I happen to be an introvert; making friends was not a problem but keeping up the conversation was. I could connect with two or three people who were like me.

I did not allow anyone in school to know I was holding on to the pain of watching my parents argue and sometimes exchange unpleasant words while they were drifting apart.

My parents were very hard working and this made it easy for us to have other people take care of us. My grandmother lived with us for a while. I would hear my parents argue and I felt there was no need for it, but I recognized it was their life and journey. I continued to eavesdrop and kept a journal based on how I felt about the situation. There were nights when I would lie on my bed and pray that God would intervene. I would cry myself to sleep. I sometimes thought that maybe having children added to their problems and I felt I was part of the reason why they fought and argued a lot.

My father was a seasoned journalist, a former editor of the Washington Post and Baltimore Sun. He was also a diplomat and was quite influential. He was always up late at night working when he was home but most of the time he was on the road. We would stay up to see him reporting from war fronts as well as other international and national events. The moment he came back, I would notice how he and my mother were drifting apart. All the gifts we were showered with could not make up for the lost times but my mother rarely showed it. She wore a smile and would sing worship songs. I could feel her pain in my soul as her voice echoed praises to God. You would never know that she was breaking on the inside.

I was very close to my mother and I could sometimes tell, due to our closeness, when something was wrong. We were never allowed to ask questions but I would go to my corner in the girls' room and lie on my bed, pray, and ask God to heal the wounds that existed in my mother's life. There were nights when I could not sleep after listening to my parents argue and all I could do was silently pray for God to intervene. I would sob and quietly wipe my tears while peeping through the coverlet. It was sometimes difficult for me to bear in school. I would run to the bathroom to cry while pretending that I needed to go, so that the teacher would not suspect something was wrong. I could not talk about the things I heard with anyone. This contributed to my introverted nature.

We would attend church on Sundays and no one seemed to notice anything, as my mother would rise to lead the choir with her sweet voice. I sometimes wondered how she managed to pull it together without anyone noticing. We would attend choir practice and bible study but deep within, I questioned God about the situation with my parents. At one point, I told God I did not believe He existed but as a child, church was a family obligation that I could not pull out from. I started challenging God as a teenager. I spent time learning the Bible and memorizing almost everything. This was part of my journey to discovering who God really is. I became more inquisitive about the Word so that I could challenge God more to prove Himself based on what I was learning about Him.

The story of Samuel was the first to stand out to me and I began to bury my head in the Book to see why God would allow so much unhappiness and pretense.

I was the emotional and sensitive child and I guess that was the reason I connected easily with all the pain around me. As I mentioned earlier, we were never allowed to confront or question our parents. After all, we are the children and we had everything so what was there to complain about? I began to develop some level of resentment towards my dad. I would look at him and sometimes wanted to scream and fight him, but then I would hold back and remind myself that I needed to show respect to my parents.

Maids took care of us when my parents were not around. There were moments when I wanted my mother or father to step in but they were not there. My grandmother lived with us for a while and I seemed to have learned so much from her. She never said much but she encouraged me with her words of wisdom. She prayed a lot as well. I once asked her about my parents and she said it was not her place to talk about it. I let it go but would go back from time to time to see if she would change her mind about talking to me. She never did. This made me turn to God with all my questions, but I guess with my vague knowledge of who God was at that time, I could not understand the process.

As time went by, I continued to withdraw into my shell as I felt so hurt by the experience and knowledge I was gaining from my parents. I began to lose confidence in myself and felt that there was nothing to live for. I allowed the pain to make me shut off at times. I continued to wonder if life was worth living. I sometimes wanted to cut myself and bleed to death, especially those times I listened to my parents argue. I never talked about it with them due to the fear instilled in us. We only observed. We were **conditioned** to be silent and I was never able to speak up about what was hurting me the most.

I remember asking my father a question once and I ended up getting punished. I would sometimes get angry and pour my heart out to my father, which made him angry and resulted in more punishment for me. I could not understand why I was sometimes punished for telling the truth. I would also sometimes wonder if my father was, in fact, my biological dad due to the way he treated me.

There were times when I wanted to ask the housemaid questions, but I was always afraid of her notifying my parents about our discussions. We would stop at my mother's office and wait until she closed from work. I would stare at my mother sitting behind her desk working away, but I never had the courage to ask her the questions that ran through my mind. This continued to eat me up inside. I became quieter and chose to keep to myself. I had learned to internalize a lot of my emotions/feelings and this would sometimes be reflected in my grades which would drop.

This silence went on for years and I continued to cry myself to sleep at night. I wondered why everything was the way it was, knowing that I was born into a family of preachers, but I guess what people observed from the outside was quite different than what we experienced on the inside (I cannot really speak for my siblings. Everyone is unique and our reactions to what was going on differed). There were days when I prayed that God would take my life but it never happened because God still had a purpose for my life.

I found a confidant in my late friend Tunde. He never asked me for anything but we talked about everything. From time to time I poured my heart out to him about everything that was going on. He was there to console me while he listened without judgment. He helped me regain my self-confidence and esteem and he was always protective of me. He was a friend of my brothers and knew how my brothers guarded their sisters. He constantly encouraged me to keep my faith in God, growing stronger each day.

There were days when I would just lay my head on his shoulders and cry, telling him how I wanted my life to end quickly. He would tell me to stop the negative thinking. Little did I know that the only person I confided in would die at a beach party. Tunde's death brought all the pain I still had buried back to surface (the pain I carried from my parent's arguments and separation). Tunde was not there to listen to me or give advice as I listened my parents argue while I pretended to be asleep. This left me with deeper pain than I envisaged.

ON BECOMING RESTORED

I got angrier with myself daily. My parents' issues on top of Tunde's death, left me with nowhere to turn. I gradually learned to numb myself to the pain and hurt while shoving everything back under the rug. I began to block out certain painful events but I could never delete them from my memory. I gradually continued to ignore anything that reminded me of the pain. This was the beginning of a conditioned lifestyle where I carried buried layers of pain. The hiding (gradual withdrawal from conversations or events) and silence, were my way of numbing myself while losing layers of awareness about who God created me to be. Instead, I was becoming the person who the world wanted me to be. I was learning to camouflage my pain in the same way my mother buried hers with a smile. I began to mirror her behavior and wore a mask while covering up my hidden layers of pain.

"Burying your pain is a form of self-hate and denial. You die to yourself, awaken the pain and suffer silently while choosing to exist rather than live."

I continued to numb myself while I kept on with my quest to discover who God really is. I was longing for answers as to why I had to go through all of these challenges. I became hungry for the knowledge of who God is and focused on studying the bible and questioning God as I longed to fill the deeper void in my life. I remember having a dream after studying the stories of Samuel and Joseph. I felt a strong force and a voice whispered to me, *"Joseph never had to understand the journey. Your life will be similar to that of Joseph but do not derail from it."* I woke up scared and I began to fear. I would sometimes laugh and wonder if the dream was real.

I sometimes got angry with my father and because of that I began to get punished and singled out. I was the one who my father would send to buy things at night. I was the one who was punished for confronting him with the truth. As I continued to experience being singled out as a child at home, I would have flashbacks of the dream and think to myself, 'What if this dream is meant to become reality?' I felt like an adopted child, or could it be that my parents gave birth to me during their most painful days? I wondered why I was punished more than the others. I thought about why I was the one connecting so much with their pain. I could not place a finger on it. I began to resent my father and the more I was punished, the more I wanted to run away from home. I felt that being vocal was not allowed but I could not hold myself back from telling him the truth about how I felt.

We sometimes connect with the pain around us while growing up and we allow what we see to condition and cloud our minds and thoughts. For me, it started with watching my parents fight and drift apart. I watched my mother being sent away for a period and we had to live at home without her. She would sometimes walk past my grandparents' home to check on us but she could not stay long. This left a void and unanswered questions that resulted in me holding on to an unfathomable level of pain. I wanted my mother to be around but I did not have control over the situation. I suffered silently knowing that her absence created a void in my life. I could not understand why she had to leave (what she had done or what she had not done). I felt I was being punished for something I did not do or know about.

"The absence of a parent can significantly affect children, especially those who are very emotional."

Reflection:
How did your childhood experience affect your adult life? Can you recall going through a situation that you may have buried underneath the rug? Did this play a part in any of your relationships as an adult, for example dating or marriage?

_____

_____

_____

_____

_____

_____

Prayer became my solace and helped to lay the foundation on which my faith was built despite my parents' separation. I struggled and almost lost faith especially when I questioned God and did not get any response. I have however, come to realize that God's timing of response is quite different from what I was *programmed* to believe.

Food for Thought:

Parents may not know how their children become affected by their actions, especially when they are facing difficult phases in their lives. They focus on what is going on with them, but not on what the child (children) may be experiencing. It is easy to ask a child if they are okay and for the child to respond back with 'yes,' but holding a deep conversation with a child allows you to know the thoughts and pain a child may be dealing with internally. As a mother, I have had to sit with my child and ask questions. Sometimes, he would not open up, so I would gently hold a conversation and eventually rephrase my question by asking him how my actions may have affected him or his growth. This has helped and continues to help us build a deeper relationship, allowing for honesty and transparency.

Every action you take as a parent leaves a positive or negative effect on your child.

Reflection:

How has your parents' relationship or actions affected phases of your life?

_____

_____

_____

_____

_____

_____

Were you able to communicate to them what you were observing and experiencing? If not, how did those things affect you as well as the choices you made or are making in life?

_____
_____
_____
_____
_____
_____

CHAPTER 2
The Polygamy Syndrome

My grandfather had more than one wife and I watched my dad pick up the same pattern. He did not marry the other women in his life but the promiscuity was there. I would sit in church on a Sunday, sing in the choir and think to myself, "Why would God allow this to happen?" I began talking to the choirmaster to find answers and he would read the Old Testament to me. He would encourage me to continue to pray and said that someday, God will answer my prayers.

There was polygamy in my father's family. This was the beginning of the conditioning of lives in our house. My dad was mirroring all he saw as a child. How can anyone blame him? This was what he observed in the family and what he grew up to know as the norm.

This is how children become conditioned and end up repeating patterns. I began to tell myself daily that this lifestyle would not be how I live. I started to lay the foundation of what I needed and what I did not want or need in my life. I started to define the kind of man I needed even though I fell off the wagon later on in my journey. The conditioning was already there and we sometimes find ourselves seeking love in places that remind us of the dad we never received love from.

I watched my dad with other women and there were days when I wanted to curse him out but I could not. He would sometimes tell us that they were people who worked for him but you can always tell when something is beyond an employee/director relationship. I began to tell myself that the opposite sex had nothing I wanted. I would still crawl into my shell at night but I had to mentally keep myself together during the day so I started learning how to become a tomboy. At one point, I told myself that I would become a nun and that it would save me from having to deal with relationship issues.

I began looking into the family history and saw that my great grandfather was also a polygamist. I detested this part of the family. Why would they pastor churches and still allow this to go on? It drew me closer to my mother as the emotional child. As an inquisitive child, I wanted to know what she was going through. I wanted to know how she felt and how she was handling things emotionally but I could not ask those questions. I only asked about her parents and she told me that her father, my maternal grandfather, was polygamous and that he died when she was young.

It was not until my healing process began that I was able to understand why she was attracted to the same environment. My maternal grandfather died when my mother was around nine years old, but she grew up with all the stepsiblings. I believe that my mother has many childhood pains that she had not healed from. I cannot truly speak for her, but as a coach, I know that this is usually the case.

My mother happens to be from a large family. One of the lessons I learned from her and her siblings and stepsiblings was that they never treated each other differently. There was no indication of who was a stepchild. They all acted as if they were from the same mother. However, on my dad's side of the family, it was different. There was a rift. Competition existed amongst them. My father shielded us from mixing with some of his family members.

This left a rage within me. I am not a supporter of polygamy by any chance. It makes me boil when I hear stories of polygamy. It has its ripple effects, generational curses that end up building a poor foundation in the family. In my parents' era, they accommodated it because they did not have a say in anything. They saw it as the norm, which led to the conditioning of a child. They went with the flow. This is one of the reasons many of us in our forties and fifties were messed up. We mirrored everything we witnessed, and internalized issues that we were not allowed to talk about. We remained silent and suffered quietly; a lot of us have experienced painful divorces and separation. We ended up carrying our parents' pains and made them ours. We did not know how to express ourselves to our parents and were not given the opportunity under threat of punishment.

Polygamy sets the pace for an unhealthy relationship. It was easy to watch some of my aunts and uncles; their friends and other family members went from one relationship to another without feeling guilty or thinking anything was wrong. Not everyone will speak out but you must realize that we become conditioned by what we see, thus developing limited beliefs that then set the pace for the lives of the children and generations to come.

This is how the pace for generational curses are set without us realizing it. We begin to think this is normal behavior and see nothing wrong with such a lifestyle but it is a complete shift from the truth and reality of life.

Polygamy does not have to be official before you call it. There are men or women who are married yet rent other homes, put these partners up and call them spouses. This was what I witnessed. My mom was the official and all the illegals were called wives. One relationship would end and my dad was with another in no time. I felt bad for my mother. She endured so much and became numb to her own life. I cannot speak for her but I continue to observe all she endured and prayed hard that I would not repeat her patterns or lifestyle. I saw it as abuse and lack of love; I would not wish it on anyone (do not get me wrong, my father was a great man but he was conditioned with this societal norm as a lifestyle).

This was how my longing for love began; I did not feel loved enough at home. I was now looking for love in the wrong places. I was longing for love and completeness. I did not know who I was and I had been conditioned by all these beliefs and experiences. I would get ideas of running away from home, my parents did not know that I was contemplating this.

My decisions back then, were based on all that I observed, and my mind was deluded...hence the wrong decisions and the wrong relationships.

The left side of the brain where judgment occurs is the same side that holds on to the negative memories, the pain, the lies; ego and fear. Hence, it is easy to make decisions based on the fear and negativity that resides with you.

As I reflect on those days, I realize that a great number of my coaching clients have gone through similar experiences. We all make decisions based on what we hold in memory or have become conditioned with. The things you may want to avoid become the very things you find yourself doing. This is because you hold on to the pain. It can be cheating on your partner because you have observed it, or because your partner reminds you of someone in the past that caused you pain. It can be repeating a parental lifestyle without realizing that you were holding on to pain from childhood.

My great grandfather and grandfather were polygamous. I also watched my father repeat the cycle. I watched some of my uncles from my maternal side do the same, as my maternal grandfather was also polygamous. I had my mind set at this point, that I was not going to live that life. I began looking for a way out. I was looking for someone to rescue me. I did not want to deal with the pain. I wanted to run away so badly. There was the material care, but the depth of love I was hoping to find from my parents was not there. They were fighting their own battles and going through their own painful periods—their seasons in life. I wanted to be loved more than I was experiencing. I felt that I was existing and not living. Their pain was oozing into my world quietly but they had no idea of the effects of it on me.

As I said in my book, *Beyond the Pain*,

"You can never love anyone when you are in pain...not even yourself."

Insight
Parents may not be aware of how their actions indirectly affect their children. We become conditioned by observing our parents, and those things we tell ourselves we would not do are the very things we tend to repeat. These lead us to look for love in the wrong places. Whether it is longing to have a partner who will shower you with the maternal/parental love you never received, or looking for a partner to rescue you from all the painful experiences you have witnessed.

Reflection:
How have your parents' actions affected or deluded you?

_____
_____
_____
_____
_____
_____
_____
_____

Did you talk to them about these or did you bottle everything up on the inside?

_____
_____
_____
_____
_____
_____

How did bottling up the pain or worries affect your growth and thought process?

_____
_____
_____
_____
_____
_____

Finding Consolation

I found consolation in a friend to whom I told everything. Tunde never crossed the line. He was a very good friend until his death. He was my shoulder to cry on and he was always quick to listen without judgment. I always looked forward to him visiting my brothers. This was my opportunity to talk to him about what was going on in my life. His death after high school (he drowned at the beach) shook me. I did not have anyone to turn to who would listen to me cry and comfort me. I did not think of turning to God at this time because I thought He did not hear my cry about my situation.

I began to grow closer to my grandfather at this point. I would go over to stay with him just to get away from home. I would sometimes ask my grandfather questions and he would respond back with, *"There are some things that are left untouched as an adult. You will understand when you get there."* He always encouraged me to be very prayerful. That was the solution I got for most of my questions. I would sometimes think, "After all, I am in high school. I may not need to know those things." I however, believe that if only we were taught those things at an early age, many would not end up in messy relationships. I believe my grandfather's generation did not know better, as they also were not taught.

CHAPTER 3

High School Days

I was privileged to have attended a Christian girls-only school. Teachers were strict; class was sometimes fun and other times painful. We had a mixture of older and younger girls. I was one of the youngest girls in my class throughout high school. My bible study teacher, Anita Roper, was one of the women who paved the way and kept me grounded in the scriptures. She grounded us with the Word of God and, daily, she encouraged us to trust Him more for everything in our lives. There were days I would go to her office for prayers.

The pain from home continued to linger in my mind but I was managing to pull myself together. I had a few close friends but they did not have an idea about what I was going through. You see, when people are friends with you on the surface, you become careful about what you share, and that was one of the reasons I kept my thoughts to myself. I sometimes would have a meltdown, go to the bathroom and sit there for a while to coordinate myself so that no one would see me cry or ask questions about what was going on.

I watched the senior girls in my class talk about dating and weekends with their boyfriends but nothing sounded interesting to me as I could not take my mind off the situation at home. Dating was the last thing on my mind based on what I had witnessed in my parents' relationship.

I would listen to some of the stories and, as an inquisitive child, I wanted to learn more but the fear of asking the seniors questions made me stay quiet.

I would watch girls scale the fence to go meet boys and I wondered about the trouble they would get into. Then came the final year of high school. I had a teacher who was pestering to date me and I kept telling him I could not. I knew all he wanted was sex and I had listened to some seniors talk about having sex with him. This teacher would whip me for coming into school late and sometimes punished me in class, but I did not budge. I was not interested in men and it was the least of my worries at that time.

I could not voice this to anyone. This was one of the experiences that ate me up inside. I kept on numbing myself while trying to keep my head up. I dreaded being late to school and seeing this teacher at the gate. I knew I was going to get whopped twice if he was at the gate. I never could share it with my friends or sister who attended the same school with me. I buckled everything on the inside and continued to wish I were no longer alive. I started to hang out more with my brothers and their friends to gain knowledge of how a man thinks and reacts to females!

I attended house parties with my brothers and got to hang out with them and their friends. This allowed me to start learning about romantic relationships, since they were dating. I was always close to my brothers' girlfriends so I could learn from them. The final year of high school came and everyone had a boyfriend but I did not want to date. There were boys who I was introduced to, but I was never interested in dating. We would meet at several school functions but the pain of watching my father treat my mother in a certain way left a bad taste in my mouth about boys and men. My mother had also instilled in us the fear of falling pregnant from a boy's touch. Her voice echoed in my mind frequently with this fear.

One of my friends had told me her brother's friend, Kay, was into me. He was a guy who girls flocked after but he was good looking. He would come around to my school after hours and try to impress me but I was not moved as I had told myself the boy thing was not happening, especially after I watched my parents argue and hurt each other with words.

I read a lot of Mills and Boon fiction novels and thought about the happily ever after. I began to imagine and long for my own happily ever after. This was a delusion that was far from reality. A friend of mine later introduced me to Kay but I was not really interested in him because he was a player. Girls were always after him and he would bring his father's car around which drew a lot of attention from the girls. As I continuously watched girls flock after Kay, I thought to myself, maybe I can be the girl in his life since he snubbed the girls who flocked after him. I decided I was going to give him a chance and promised to let him know at a house party we both attended. We used to communicate through little written notes back then. I had given the note to a friend to give to him and I looked forward to meeting him at the house party. We met and attended several parties together.

As a very attractive woman (and I still am - giggling), I always had a boy's attention. I used it then as an edge to learn more about boys. I remember one of boys chasing me back then cursing me out after dancing with him. He gently whispered dirty words in my ears and I usually told him if he would have his sister do the same thing, he wanted to engage me in, then he can come back to ask me to do the same. He silently whispered curse words in my ears and I burst out laughing.

I learned how to use my beauty as a weapon to torture boys, but then I had to face the toughest times of my life, saying 'yes' to a guy and 'no' to myself while letting go of the principles I held on to for so long. Kay was a ladies' man. He was also very attractive and the moment I realized that the girls were flocking after him, I decided to give being his 'babe' a shot. It all started with the forehead and lip kisses and hugs at the initial stage.

Kay would make sexual advances but I told him I was not interested in sex, as I had promised myself that I would remain pure by abstaining. He tried to convince me on several occasions but each time I would call off the relationship. He would come back pleading that he did not mean to put pressure on me. I would forgive him and go back to the relationship.

He organized his birthday party and wanted me to be there. On his birthday, I could hear my spirit (what some call intuition) telling me not to go to his party but I thought to myself, "All those girls will be there, I have to show up and pull the 'girlfriend stunt.'" I got dressed in a blue stripped-off shoulder dress with a long side slit.

Upon my arrival, he asked me to follow him to his parents' room to get more drinks for the party. I innocently followed without knowing what was going to happen. Then he asked me to look behind the sofa in his parents' room for a bag. I bent over to check the bags behind the sofa. As I raised my head up, I noticed Kay was standing half naked. He had a gun in his hand and told me to get undressed. He flaunted it and said, 'This is my dad's gun.' I did not know what to think. I wondered if it was real or fake. I tried to argue and he told me he could pull the trigger. My heart rate increased and I became extremely nervous. He walked me over to the bed and told me again to get undressed. I began to cry and pleaded with him. He placed the gun next to my head while holding on to it. I was not sure if the gun was loaded so I succumbed, and told me to open my legs wide. I submitted with the gun pointing at me while keeping quiet and obeying his orders.

After raping me, he inserted a pill into me and told me that I would not get pregnant. I told him I wanted to go home and he called a cab to drop me off. My friend (who had gone to the party with me and had no idea what had happened to me) and I left in the cab but I never told her what happened to me. I got home and puked several times. I took a shower, threw away my underwear and took several tablets of Valium to sleep. I did not want to wake up again...I wanted to die. I was sick to my stomach and could not tell anyone about what had just happened to me. I would take several Valium tablets every night thinking I could take my life but it never happened. I would sneak some of my father's alcoholic drinks in a cup into my room and drink myself to sleep. I had nightmares about the rape for days. I would wake up in the night and stare at the ceiling while sobbing quietly. I had flashback after flashback and insomnia began to kick in.

Kay did not give up after the incident. He came back time after time to see me and wanted more. He would shower me with gifts and continued to make demands. I did not know what to do but listen to him. He threatened me and told me that no one would believe my story if I decided to speak out. He reminded me of how many people liked him and why they would believe him over me. He told me that he did it because he cared about me and wanted to be with me. This left me really confused, as I was naïve. I would sometimes look at him in fear, as I did not know what he was capable of, especially after pointing a gun at me. The fear he instilled in me left me listening to him and following his orders. I would sometimes panic at the sound of his voice and give in to whatever he asked me to do.

I did not know if anyone would believe me if I spoke out. I did not know what he could do to me if I spoke about the incident with anyone. I had to live with the fear and pain and it made me withdraw more into my shell. I counted down until my next period and when I finally saw my cycle, I breathed relief. I continued to have flashbacks, waking up sweating and silently crying myself to sleep without anyone knowing.

I started to listen to music and stay in my room to block

out the opportunity of having a conversation with anyone. I would pretend I was asleep after school and homework but the hurt and memories of the rape haunted me for months and years. I began to get involved in church activities to avoid thinking about it (as a way to also numb myself). I even thought of running away from home as I continued to have flashbacks; I did not want my parents to find out about the incident.

After the incident, I went to stay with my grandfather for a while, as I did not want my parents to suspect that something had happened to me. I continued to drink myself to sleep and kept taking several Valium tablets every night to numb myself from the memories but they never went away. I gradually began suppressing them and continued to do so when I went to college. I slowly began making new friends but the pain was still there and I could not hold long conversations about relationships.

I went back several times and at one point, I approached Kay to ask him why he had raped me, as it had messed me up completely. I would attend parties and see him but I would turn away quickly or leave the party to avoid making contact with him. This ate me up inside for such a long time that I began to detest men.

I had yielded to peer pressure and dated, and it had ended up in me being raped (choices and consequences). If I had remained true to myself, no such thing would have happened. I had to learn this lesson the hard way. I had to live in pretense after the pain. I felt lost and empty. The most important piece of me had been stripped from me!

Reflection:

How did peer pressure contribute to your choices? What did you learn from yielding to peer pressure? How much pain did it bring and what did you do about the pain?

_____
_____
_____
_____
_____
_____

_____

"The fog may seem thick but the sun will surely pierce through and brighten up the sky. Allow yourself to continue to rest on the wings of God's love and watch yourself learn to soar high."

CHAPTER 4
College Days

As I began my college years, I was in so much pain from my rape and from my childhood experiences. I began to smoke and to drink alcohol (especially champagne) to further numb my pain. My roommate did not have a clue why I kept so much to myself at times.

I had more male friends than females as I continued my quest for knowledge about the opposite sex. My friend, SR and I talked a lot. We grew closer and started to share personal experiences. I would pray with him as well as encourage him from time to time. We began to hang out a lot but his mother was not a big fan. She usually called me to the corner (sometimes in church) and reminded me that she was his mom. She would tell me that as long as she was alive, her son and I would never be together.

I frequently told him what his mother said but it only made us grow somewhat closer. We hung out and talked often until he traveled out of the country.

At this point, I was now back to square one. The feeling of rejection swamped over me. No one to talk to about my pain any longer. I kept using smoking and drinking as my comfort and soother. My grades dropped badly as I could not focus or talk to anyone about what I was going through deep inside...my thought process had been messed up!

I had lecturers who wanted to have sexual relationships with me but I was not interested. Sometimes, I ended up with lower grades for refusing to sleep with them. I would go home frustrated and could not talk about my ordeal in college. I ended up flunking and had to repeat a few classes.

I continued to long for a way to fill the void in my life. I wanted to stay far away from home because of what my parents were going through. However, after flunking college I had to move back home before starting another college. I decided to move to my grandfather's home as I did not get along with my dad. I also did not want to watch my mother suffer silently. I wanted to be far away where I could focus and improve on my grades.

I started a new college and continued to push harder to keep my head above the waters. One of my lecturers back in college, Mr. A, began to help me over my "escape" from pain (i.e., champagne, Guinness, and cigarettes consumed for comfort; this is how addiction begins for some people). He would share the scriptures with me and I would have to exchange my cigarettes for biscuits. After a while, I began to exchange my biscuits for chewing gum and I eventually quit smoking cold turkey.

I had bad asthma attacks when I was smoking, but no one discovered that the cigarettes were sending me into panic/wheezing mode. God did not only place Mr. A in my path as a lecturer in college but also as my purpose helper to help me overcome some of things I was hiding behind. He continued to mentor me while in college and I will never forget those days.

Why I Was Choosing the Wrong Partners

I went off for an internship at one of the hospitals in Lagos and met Mike. We ran into each other on the stairway and our eyes locked. I wanted to know who he was. I asked a few friends in the hospital but no one knew him. One afternoon, I went to pick up my lunch from the hospital kitchen and once again ran into Mike. He invited me to sit down and have lunch. We began talking and we immediately connected as we ate lunch together.

I went up to HR one day, to submit a document and ran into the HR manager (who was more like a family member). She called me into her office and told me that she and Mike had had several conversations about me. She treated me like a sister; she was like family to me. She encouraged me to build on the friendship with Mike quietly and outside of work. Mike and I became closer over time. We were like five and six. It was not too long before a few co-workers in the hospital discovered. We brightened up each other's days and lives. We began dating and I eventually met his parents. His dad liked me a lot but I could not really tell what his mother thought. She was quiet and hardly talked to me much. Mike's siblings and I also became close. He attended parties held by my family (and vice versa) and everyone in his family got along with me. I fell in love with him (it was not genuine love...it was the infatuation and lust kind of love).

We would hang out on weekends and we were inseparable. We made each other laugh and cry, and I would often help him cook meals while spending time with him (now that I have become a coach, I encourage single women today, not to give away this wifey duty). Our friends believed that the relationship was heaven made. Mike's sister and I were very close and attended the same college. Mike and I shared everything with each other—we kept no secrets!

Mike moved into his own place after a while. We would have friends over on weekends and both of us would cook and clean up after entertaining friends. I thought I had found my happily ever after and my escape from home. However, Mike had hidden plans and he could not find a way to tell me that he was leaving the country. I left campus one weekend to go see Mike. Upon arrival at his apartment, I noticed his mother was outside packing his things into a car. I approached her to find out what was going on and she notified me that he had left the country. We had had a few arguments back and forth and even called it quits for a while but we were so much into each other that we were eventually back together within a short period. This did not give me a clue that Mike was traveling, neither did he discuss it with me.

"Never think someone is your forever, especially if they cannot keep you informed on all matters."

My heart sank. I could not believe what was happening. I felt rejected and lost. I stopped by at a friend of ours to ask if he knew that Mike was traveling and he said he thought I was aware. I went back to campus sobbing. My heart was broken. I thought about all the "why" questions but nothing seemed to come to mind. For days, I felt lost in thoughts and short of words. The man who I thought was going to rescue me had just dumped me. I had expectations that were never met. I had long sleepless nights I could never account for; staying awake and thinking deeply.

I started to focus on getting back to studying and hoping for the best grades possible. My initial feeling that I did not need a man came back to mind but I still felt the need to fill the void and get rid of the pain I had buried inside. I continued to struggle with the layers of pain I now had in my heart and life.

Not too long after the ordeal with Mike, I met Abi through a friend. I had met him before while in my first year of college but I gave him such a hard time. He would drive several miles across states, to come visit me and I would tell him I was not interested. Abi never gave up and a while after his persistence, I decided it was time to move on (from my heartbreak) so I gave him a chance. I felt since Mike was now out of the picture, giving Abi a chance would solve my problems and take away my loneliness. We started dating and I fell in love with his family. They were so pleasant (and are still so loving even today) and welcoming but there was something about his mother; she and I were not connecting. We hung out at his aunt's a lot more than his parents'.

Abi and I lost each other for a short while but I got back in contact with him after meeting at a friend's party. Abi and I were like five and six. His aunt was like a second mother back then. We spent a lot of time together and with his family. He would drive down to see me in college from another state and I grew much closer to him than anyone else. We were off and on due to his cheating habits (which I guess were as a result of being young and having no sense of purpose). I was very principled and always laid down rules but he would break them. Not knowing who I was, I was quick to forgive him and let him back into my life. I thought Abi and I were meant to be. His siblings and cousins were like my family. No one could tell we were not really blood relatives. Some of his friends are now my close friends and we all still keep in touch. Abi and I were together for eight years and through him, I met my "to be husband." Abi pleaded, promising to change if I would give him another chance but I was bent on moving forward.

I had to call it quits after Abi cheated again. He came to apologize to me when he introduced me to my ex-husband but I was tired of the cheating habits and did not want him back in my life. We were both infatuated with each other and deep in lust while thinking it was love. As I look back at that experience (spending eight years together), I realized that Abi's role in my life was to teach me those things I did not want my God-given spouse to do: Cheat, have casual sex with multiple partners, lie about the relationship and be a player. Those were not qualities I needed in a man who I was going to spend the rest of my life with. I discovered those were the things my father did and I had told myself that I did not need them in a partner.

However, I was drawn to those very things because I was operating in the subconscious and unconscious space. I had become conditioned with those things I did not want in a man. Coupled with my pain, these things stuck with me and led to me seeking the wrong partners. I wanted a man who was like my father but not a man with his habits. Hence, I found myself meeting and dating the same type of men because I was looking for a father figure in a husband. The truth and reality are that you can never marry your father. Hence, you should never look for a man like your father but look for a man who knows you are his missing rib and whom you belong to.

I did not fully understand what Abi's purpose in my life was until I found myself. This is why we need to know everyone's purpose in our lives before getting into any type of relationship.

"You will never be a rib too short or too long to bruise each other badly but you will fit in your place as God deemed it to be."

I kept looking for the wrong partners because I had so much pain and had not healed completely. If you do not completely grieve and heal from your past, you will only attract potential partners who carry similar pain/trauma. Always remember that pain attracts pain. They will raise your awareness of the things you need to heal from but you will only think they came to break you further.

I was choosing men who reminded me of my rape and of my father's polygamous lifestyle. I was looking for them to take away the pain they did not give to me. I did not understand at that time what trauma bond was at that time.

Trauma bond occurs as a result of ongoing abuse that is coupled with intermittent reward and punishment that creates emotional bonds (which makes the individual hold on and find it hard to let go of the partner). Instead healing, I was attracting more pain due to the trauma bond, I was acquiring more pain and building up the more layers of pain, while losing myself.

Reflection:
What choices on relationships were based on your relationship with your father or mother?

___

___

___

___

___

What did you learn from your parents' relationship or what did you observe that may have affected your choice of partner(s)?

___

___

___

___

___

___

"Knowing everyone's purpose in your journey is vital to your growth. You may think that people are there to accept you but without knowing their purposes, you will lose out on some of the blessings God has for you."

CHAPTER 5
The Quest for Love

I began working at a hospital where my grandfather was a member of the board. The family connection allowed me to quickly obtain employment in the laboratory where I had completed my internship. This was the same hospital where Mike and I met (and also the same hospital where I met my ex-husband).

Going back to work at the hospital brought back memories of Mike. However, I was determined to focus on work and leave the past behind me. I began to ignore people who brought back conversations about Mike. I did not care about what they had to say. Abi was also no longer in my life at this point. I was back to being single. I was not interested in a relationship as I was tired of drama.

I stopped on my way from work one day at a new store that opened on Allen Avenue. I wanted to see what they had to offer and also to get a gift for a friend's birthday. As I was staring at several items on a shelf, the manager approached me and introduced himself. Abbey and I began to chat outside the store while I waited for a cab. We ended up exchanging information.

Waiting for a cab to take me to work one morning I noticed Abbey driving out from across the street. I did not realize he lived so close to my house. He offered to drop me off at work. Once again, I began to draw close to a man with my father's name.

Abbey did not tell me he was in a serious relationship. He lied to me about his relationship with the other woman. I found out and confronted him and he told me he was more interested in me. At this time, I was not hearing from God about everything that was happening to me. I was allowing my emotions to lead me into the wrong places. I ventured out to date a Muslim in my quest to find answers to my problems.

I spent a lot of time around Abbey and wanted him to rescue me from all of my pain. He showered me with gifts which added to the clouds that I was already experiencing. I lost the ability to see clearly the drive to find quick answers and short cuts to my problems kept leading me into the arms of the wrong partners.

One of my friends was getting married to Abbey's friend and I could once again hear my intuition tell me I should not attend the wedding but I turned a deaf ear (I had not yet learned how to listen to my intuition). Abbey's long-time girlfriend showed up and caused a scene. I had to leave the wedding. I felt so embarrassed about what had happened. Abbey came back to apologize and I was too quick to forgive once again.

I had introduced one of my little sisters from church to Abbey and he had helped her secure a job at his sister's store in Ikeja (where he served as the manager). She told me I was in the wrong relationship and needed to put an end to it. I did not listen to her as this was my way of rebelling against God. It was me trying to learn about another religion outside of what I know. It was me trying to see if the Muslim principles would give me answers. Little did I know I was getting myself into more trouble than I needed.

After several months, I called it quits with Abbey after having a conversation with his girlfriend and sister and ended a phase of several dramatic incidents. I was not looking for drama or derailment. I discovered I was continuing to seek for answers in the wrong places.

I did not get the answers I needed from God, though I was learning the Muslim way from Abbey. I learned to read the Quran and pray the Muslim way but I did not feel any better and I became more bitter.

"One of the reasons I kept going down the wrong route was that I was choosing to date men with my father's name...I was trying to create a relationship with my father through other men (based on the one I never had with him that left the void in my life)."

Looking back now, I see that those wrong partners, made me realize that I did not love myself enough. I did not know that I, myself, was enough. Hence, I did not know or understand how to get the answers I needed or how to gain clarity. My past relationships, all with the wrong partners, were never built on a foundation of love. We were only infatuated or we sometimes, focused on the lustful part of the relationship.

Reflection:

As a single or divorced man/woman, have you noticed yourself choosing someone based on your relationship with your father or mother in your past relationships?

_____
_____
_____
_____
_____

What were the missing pieces of the puzzle in the relationship with your father or mother that led you to the men/women in your past relationships?

_____
_____
_____
_____
_____
_____

Not too long after the relationship with Abbey ended, I ran into Abi again after many years apart. We got talking and made plans to meet at his aunt's the following weekend. The spark was still very much there and it was quickly rekindled when we met over the weekend.

Abi's sense of humor always made it easy for me to forgive and reconnect with him. I always wanted that in a man. Abi would stop by my office at the hospital to visit and would sometimes pick me up from work. We kept seeing each other and attending family events. I grew much closer to his cousins and aunt as time went by.

The lust and infatuation grew deeper and I was once again looking for someone to rescue me from home. I was longing for the fatherly love I never had, with the hope of finding it in a partner.

Our relationship was intermittent due to the principles/standards I did not wish to compromise.

As we began to get better and deeper in our relationship, Abi told me that he was traveling out of the country and did not know when he would return. My heart was once again broken. Abi told me not to worry and that he was going to stay in touch with me.

Communication was great for the first few months after which he ghosted. I visited his aunt and she told me he had moved on. I went home sobbing and thought to myself, "Maybe *I am not meant to be with a man.*"

Abi returned to Nigeria after a year; little did I know he was with another woman.

Abi's aunt had invited me to the family event while we were at her house. He mentioned that he spoke to me about the event and believed I had forgotten. I decided to attend the event but on getting there, I found Abi with another woman. I stared at him and the new woman for a while. I felt like a fool and gathered myself together, then decided to leave the event. I should have never given him the opportunity to make me an option.

This was one of the things I realized during my healing process. I was making myself an option in the quest to find answers to my own problems. I was looking for a rescuer, yet forgetting that God was the Only One who could rescue me from all my fears and pain.

Reflection:
How many times have you allowed yourself to be an option while trying to stay with someone who was not making you a priority or treating you as he/she would treat themselves?

_____

_____

_____

_____

_____

Abi later came to my office to apologize. That was the day he introduced me to my ex-husband. I was still broken and hurt, and yet made another irrational decision to jump into a new relationship. I did not know any better. I was still on my quest to get away from the pain at home and to run away in order to find love on my own. It all started on lustful grounds and infatuation. I had no idea of what commitment was about at that age. I was seeking commitment but I was not yet committed to myself.

> *"Never seek commitment with someone without learning about and becoming committed to yourself."*

During this time, I decided to go and stay with my cousin in Victoria Island. Things were still the same at home and I wanted to be far away from the stress of watching my parents go at each other. I also worked my transfer to the Surulere branch of the hospital where I was working.

I did not want anyone to discover what had happened to me, or to have an idea of the pain I was dealing with (the shame). I ran into Kay once again. He had also moved to Victoria Island. I had another friend, who I will refer to as Andy, who I had informed about my ordeal with Kay. He and Kay were neighbors. I told Andy about Kay because he noticed I was always avoiding him. Andy set up a group to beat Kay up and later told me. At that point, I had to leave my cousin's place. I did not know what Kay could do. I avoided attending Andy's parties (including his engagement party and wedding) so that I would not run into Kay.

I was now on the run. I was running away from the person who had left me with the trauma and also from a friend who was defending me in the process. I had to go back to live with my parents once again. I worked my transfer back to the mainland since I was back at my parents'.

Reflection
How has a childhood trauma affected your life and friendship with others?

_____
_____
_____
_____
_____
_____

I resumed work at the Ikeja branch of the hospital. I kept going to work at and talking to my ex-husband on phone frequently. I did not like the long-distance relationship at all. One day, my ex-husband called to ask if I would marry him. I immediately said yes. I thought since we were always talking about most things and had so much in common, this was it for me. Both families met at the traditional 'introduction' that was planned and agreed upon. My mother and sister had suggested it took place.

My family wanted me to have an elaborate wedding, but I was not up for it. My ex-husband came back to Nigeria briefly and we went to the marriage registry so that I could obtain a visa and join him in the US.

It was my third day in the US when I realized I might have made the wrong choice for my life but I had no option to go back. I spoke with my mother about it and she said I could not return home. I sometimes felt lost while staying at home and not working. I was not prepared for what I had ventured into.

I decided to get a phlebotomy certification that allowed me to get back into the laboratory and to rejoin the workforce.

CHAPTER 6
The Workforce

The workforce was a bit challenging. I remember God speaking to my heart before leaving Nigeria on not compromising who I am with what I think I want. Every time I faced a contradictory situation, the Holy Spirit would remind me not to compromise my being. The medical field, however, brought those conflicts across my path, and I had to choose between passing the test of my faith or falling away from it all.

I began working at a medical laboratory as a medical technician/phlebotomist in New York. It was routine for me to get into work and pray before I began my duties. I had to prepare my mind and disconnect from the world to allow God to use me wherever He placed me. I usually arrived at work 10 minutes early so that I could have enough time to pray in the closet within the laboratory. My supervisor would get angry every time she found me praying. I was not praying loudly but silently sitting with my hands together and my head slightly bowed. The more she became uncomfortable, the more I felt something was not right. The Holy

Spirit began to stir me to pray more, and I continued to ask God to reveal what was dark in that laboratory and why He had led me there.

On the morning when things began to unravel, I could not believe what I saw. My supervisor was drawing blood from an eight-year-old, but she could not find her veins. She tried twice and was unsuccessful. She asked the girl and her mother to wait outside in the lobby, saying that she would call them back for another attempt. She called in the next patient and took blood from him. She collected extra tubes from the man but did not label the tubes. She then invited the young girl back in and pretended to collect blood but could not find her vein again to draw blood from. She removed the needle, grabbed the unlabeled tubes that she had collected from the man, and placed the labels with the girl's name onto the tubes.

My heart began to race. I began to think. "Oh, Lord, why would someone do this?" I watched her the same day repeat the same thing with two patients. Part of me wanted to stay silent so that I could keep my job but God reminded me that He had brought me there for a purpose: To expose the wickedness this woman had been perpetrating for years.

I decided to talk to my colleagues, who had all been there for years before I was employed, and some of them told me that they had known for over seven years. I began to weep. I could not believe what I was hearing. I took it upon myself to notify upper management. I was asked if I had enough evidence to prove my statements. I asked the center administrator to invite the girl back for a repeat blood sample. The following day, the girl was called back to the center, and one of the doctors collected the blood specimens. The results came back with the evidence. She was being treated for cancer, but she never had cancer. This was because the lab manager was busy swapping samples of several patients. How could such wickedness happen before one's eyes yet some decided to keep quiet? Where is the love and "treating others as you wanted to be treated?" How can someone go home and sleep after such atrocities?

I returned to the closet where I normally pray—my little "war room" in the office. On stepping out from the closet, my colleagues relayed the news that my supervisor had been terminated (after 35 years of working at the center). Imagine her doing the dirty work for all those years.

I had peace within, and I told my colleagues that I would likely be terminated and I believed that my work was done. My purpose was fulfilled in that place. A week later, I got to work, and my colleagues told me that when my former supervisor's office had been cleaned out, Voodoo dolls with pins were brought out from the drawers under her desk.

I never used to believe in those things until I started to see them and had a personal encounter. She had brought her wickedness to the medical institution. I began to think of the number of people who may have died or wrongly diagnosed with diseases they never had. But there were also those who had worked with her and kept quiet in order to keep their jobs.

Two weeks after she was terminated, the organization laid me off. I was at peace with it because I knew my purpose there was complete.

Question: Do you know your purpose where God has placed you?

_____
_____
_____
_____
_____
_____

Are you becoming frustrated because your agenda has not come to fruition, yet you still fail to see the reason why God took you there? Have you ever fulfilled your purpose in a relationship, job or place that God took you through, and did you gain knowledge through that process?

_____
_____
_____
_____
_____
_____

Yet Another Encounter:
A week after I was laid off, I was hired by another prestigious medical center in New York City. I began to work in the laboratory, and my spirit once again jolted me, advising me not to get too comfortable, as this was another assignment. I would pray each time I stepped into my cubicle and ask God to allow me to see what I was there to do...my purpose.

Two weeks into the job, I was called into my supervisor's office to explain a new position she wanted me to take on. It was a new research program for an Ashkenazi Jewish genetic disease. I would be assisting the doctors calling patients who were pregnant (once we discovered through the lab reports) and had an unborn child who carried the genetic disease. The calls were to invite them back, and the pregnancy would be terminated to prevent them from giving birth to or raising the child.

I was trusting God for the fruit of the womb during this period. I knew right away that this was another test of my faith and of my walk with God. I knew this was another way to expose what was dark and bring it to light. I could not do this. I refuse to be part of a murder. I refuse to support killing the unborn child who may not end up having the disease. I knew what prayer could do. I knew I would have to compromise who I was if I agreed to take this task on. I would be selling my birthright. I told my supervisor I could not take on the job. I walked out of the office and went home rather than returning to my desk. I got back home and I began to cry. I had to make a tough decision to quit my job even though I needed the money. My life and purpose were bigger than the temporary want I had: Money.

It would be easy to go for the money and earn the salary but I had to go home to sleep with the thought of the children being killed. These people did not create those children; they were God's gift to those parents. They may have ended up not having that disease. I was once again torn on the inside, but I knew I had made the best decision. I thought to myself, "Do I please myself, or please God? Do I fill temporary wants, only to lose my hold on my salvation?" I called my supervisor the following morning and told her I was not coming back to work. She responded that I would never be employed in that organization again. I told her my God-given assignment there was complete and I was in a happy place. I later volunteered to work in the medical laboratory at the organization to gain some skills. After a month of voluntary work, I was offered a position with a medical group as a medical laboratory manager. I never thought that I would be elevated, but I stood my grounds during the test and refused to compromise my faith.

My faith had been tested, and God was elevating me for not compromising who He created me to be. I had only suffered pain every time I compromised. I was depleted from my "true essence" when I chose to give in. I was taken back to an unhappy place to fulfill temporary desires that would not last a lifetime — this time I chose to stand. I decided to win (although to some, it will seem like a failure). I allowed God to take me through while holding on to His Promises.

"When you go through deep waters, I will be with you. When you go through rivers of difficulty, you will not drown. When you walk through the fire of oppression, you will not be burned up; the flames will not consume you."

Why do we find it hard to go through the rivers of difficulty but we are not able to hold on to God's Word? He will never allow us to drown. The truth is that we have been

ON BECOMING RESTORED

taught what to think, not how to think. We have been made to believe the lies that look too good to be true, just as Eve fell in the Garden of Eden. We believe in the sugar-coated fast lane, but forget that the gate back to God is narrow, not wide.

Where are you currently in your life? Are you finding yourself along your journey, and how are you learning to get back on track when you slip, or when you compromise who you are?

_____

_____

_____

_____

_____

_____

CHAPTER 7
The Journey Continues

I spent a few months volunteering at the Microbiology Lab at Mount Sinai hospital in New York to build up my skills. I learned as much as I could and met some great co-workers and managers. After a few months of volunteering, I secured a full-time position as a medical lab manager.

As the Lab Manager, not only did I increase the profits for the medical group but also trained others to become better at what they do. The laboratory did not bring in much income prior to my employment; I was there to help them increase revenue. This was part of my journey to having an impact in that group. There was also the exposure of the medical technologist who claimed to have a degree but did not.

I left the organization as I had to relocate. I was offered opportunities to go back. However, I believe that my purpose there was done. God only takes us to a place for a reason, and when that assignment is over, you cannot return there.

Food for Thought:
Every time I try to go there (compromise my faith), God awakens me to the reasons why He continues to open my eyes to see the truth. Ask yourself the question, "If you are truly grounded in God and walking in purpose, who deviates: God or you?" If it is God, it will never be the way things are done in the world. He will remind you always that you are a light.

Reflection:
How often have you forgotten about who and whose you are? How often do you recognize the tests of your faith along your journey in life?

_____
_____
_____
_____
_____
_____
_____
_____

"Without understanding the season you are in, you will not recognize the faith elevation or testing phases. You will easily compromise who you are in favor of becoming the person others want you to be."

After living in Mississippi for a few years, it was time to relocate. I began praying and asking God for guidance as to where to go, and I selected three states. I prayed about the three states, and I received confirmation for Maryland.

I wanted to secure a position before the move, and God opened the doors for me to get a job. I started working as a software developer for a company in Fairfax VA. I did not realize how far Fairfax, VA was from Columbia, MD and had to quit my job to work as a consultant in Maryland as I got tired of the commute. I secured a contracting job with a consulting company and later moved to work for an IT firm in Glen Burnie, MD.

The Corporate Fraud

I began working as a consultant for an IT firm in Glen Burnie, MD.

I was a bit hesitant when I started working with the organization. I would pray and ask God to reveal my purpose at this company (just as I had done everywhere else, I had worked). Everything seemed odd when I started working there. There were hidden secrets and no one wanted to answer questions when I asked them. The more I prayed, the more my spirit prompted me not to compromise who I was.

The day finally arrived when things were brought to light. I sat behind my desk working on tasks assigned to me. I was called by one of the managers into a brief meeting. He handed me some documents to work on and mistakenly included a document that contained my forged signature. The document was an eye opener.

My signature had been forged on a contract proposal. I looked at the document closely and I could not believe my eyes. I had never been presented with the document. No one mentioned the contract. I made a copy of the document and I took a walk outside the office before I headed back to my desk.

I went into the document repository and found the folder containing the soft copy (computer digital version). I decided to see what else was in that document folder. As I opened the documents, one by one, I found forged signatures of former and current employees on several documents. My heart began to race. How can a CEO do this? Why would he and his partner go to this extent? What is the world turning into? This is pure fraud! This is how some organizations use employee information without consent. This is what greed does. Greed is idolatry, and when you do not know where to draw the boundaries, you begin to take advantage of others using your power which is, more often than not, driven by ego.

I did not realize at this point that God was taking me to places in order to let me understand that not every door that is opened is from Him. God was allowing me to see the reasons why I need NOT compromise myself and my faith with the things of the world. God was making me aware that I cannot conform to the standards of the world; I have to constantly be transformed by the renewing of my mind. This was the end of my assignment at the organization. I brought the matter to the attention of the owner but he denied it and threatened me.

Food for Thought:

Have you ever found yourself working for an organization where you discovered or uncovered unethical behavior?

_____
_____
_____
_____
_____
_____

Did you keep quiet without realizing that God had opened your eyes to a particular situation?

_____
_____
_____
_____
_____
_____

Did you compromise by choosing to stay silent (knowing it was wrong)?

_____
_____
_____
_____
_____
_____

How did it affect/alter your character (in terms of leading you to begin accepting lying as a choice)?

_____
_____
_____
_____
_____
_____

I went on to work at several other organizations. Then came the next job.

I took on this new job with excitement. I was so elated when my supervisor told me that the owner of the company had requested that I work with him on a project. I had only been there for two weeks. I was yet to meet him but most of the management team members had walked up to my office and had told me about the news. The project meetings kicked off smoothly. I was the only one there in the meetings with him; we had the aim of winning a contract worth almost $12 million. A week or two after the meetings, the good news arrived.

The contract was awarded. I stepped up above and beyond without the business development team to support the owner with winning the contract. I engaged in a conversation with him about not being brought into the company for the contract and how I needed to be compensated for the work done on winning the project. All I received was a resounding 'no.' Greed once again showed up in my eyes but I was not moved. They were only showing me how they rolled but I knew God was preparing me for something greater. I put in my resignation and walked out the door. That chapter was closed.

CHAPTER 8
More Challenges

I got a job in July 2014 with a native American company, and I knew it was God who had taken me there for a reason and a season. Everything began smoothly, but we all know that nothing can be smooth all the way. I knew I was there for a purpose. God favored me and allowed me to get a great vacation package that created room for me to travel on God-given assignments. After a year, I was transferred to another division of the organization as a lead. Everything seemed alright until the new manager stepped in: Another trial phase—a season of my journey was about to begin.

The dynamics of the team and the project changed. I found myself with a manager who took me through another difficult season of testing my faith. At this time, I was now healed and in a deeper relationship with God so my emotions could no longer cloud my judgment. I was now able to recognize someone in pain (who may also have been a test or distraction) who may not have been living consciously and may have been unaware of his or her actions.

I had been going through my recovery process and receiving transfusion. (I had lost five pints of blood during and after my separation and divorce). I had to send this manager pictures of me undergoing transfusion while he demanded I showed up for meetings (this violated the Privacy Act and HIPAA policies). I immediately notified the HR director by forwarding my email with a picture of me undergoing transfusion so I could have this on record. Talk about having a manager on the other side! I managed to show up at work when I felt a bit stronger.

I had taken several government training courses, and as someone who is ethical, I do not break the rules. My program manager wanted me to stick with him and take information out of the government environment. I told him on several occasions that I would not do anything unethical. Every time I refused to compromise, he would leave me out of meetings and write me up as not cooperating with management. He continued to look for ways to eliminate me from the team. He would leave me out of meetings and claim that I had not turned up. I would send requests for the meeting invites, and he would only respond when I notified the client in order to get involved.

I fell ill during this period but did not know how severe it was. I discovered I had a tumor during my annual checkup. I noticed my stomach growing bigger on one side and could not imagine what was happening. I was getting closer to 50 so I thought it could be hormonal. At this point, I began struggling with walking and I had to drive in excruciating pain to work as my operations manager, as well as my program manager, took away my privilege to work from home.

My program manager told me that if I did not report to work, I was going to be fired. I was currently under medical care and needed to hold on to my medical insurance. Despite being advised medically to remain on bed rest, I got into my car the next day for a meeting at Bethesda, MD. The traffic was horrible, and I had to stop twice along the drive to throw up.

It took me almost two and a half hours to get to work. By the time I got there, I was bleeding profusely and could barely walk. I managed to park my car and walk to the building where we were stationed. I took the elevator to the third floor but could no longer move as the pain had worsened. I held on the walls and at a point began to crawl. I would get up at intervals and walked while half bent over into the office. At this point, I thought I was going to black out.

I managed to compose myself for the client's meeting (as I had to lead the meeting). After the meeting was over, a woman who worked for the client, walked up to me and said, "*You look very frail. You should not be here.*" I managed to smile, and I told her I was going to be okay.

The bleeding had increased, and I had to rush to the restroom to change my clothes. On my way back, one of the client's employees approached me and said that I needed to leave the premises, as they did not want me to become a medical liability.

My program manager began to stare at me and I could tell from the look in his eyes that he was not going to allow me to go home. The client representative called for a wheelchair and ordered that I be provided with the government laptop and sent home. She wheeled me to pick up and sign for the laptop and asked that someone escort me out of the building. As I was leaving, I told my program manager that I had been authorized by the client to work remotely until I recovered. He looked at me and said, "*You better be here tomorrow!*" I immediately called the HR director to notify her of the situation.

I was placed on a medication to shrink the tumor so that I could have surgery, and I resumed bedrest. My surgery went well but I had to get on the laptop three days afterwards as my program manager kept sending me email messages to provide information about one thing or another. I continued to deal with excruciating pain. I once again had to notify the HR manager, and she advised that I sign off and get some rest. I logged off and called my doctor's office to complain about the pain. It was the same pain I had before surgery. My doctor provided me with a note stating that I needed to be off work for the next two days. My program manager did not stop sending emails to request information. One of my colleagues notified me that my program manager had mentioned at work that he did not believe I had undergone surgery.

I could not apply for another job due to my medical condition, so I continued to endure while working hard to recover. I worked from home for a few months while on the Federal Medical Leave Act (FMLA) and the program manager got on my case once again. He requested that I report to the Columbia office where I could not work with the government laptop. My colleagues noticed that I could barely walk and one of them took it upon herself to take me home. I worked hard to meet program manager's demands, as I needed the medical coverage while recuperating.

The vice president and program manager would call meetings and have me document minute by minute activities for my assigned tasks. They told me the client had requested the information. Whenever I asked the client representative if this was true, she would tell me that she had never requested such a thing. I also began to document everything that was transpiring, as I knew the program manager and the vice president were trying hard to get rid of me.

I knew this was another test of my faith (based on where I was in my journey with God) so I was not moved emotionally because I recognized that emotions are given to us to help us find our way back to God for directions. I continued to pray to God and favor came through the client. I was granted permission to continue to work remotely.

I was homebound for four months, but this was a season God used to separate and prepare me for what He had planned. I was also scheduled for several speaking engagements but I had to cancel everything. During this season, God led me to speak at an event and I discovered that several people there needed the message. I also received an award that I did not see coming. The award was not about me but about what God was doing.

I had to halt work on my third book and learned to trust God on a deeper level. Amid the storm, I remained calm as God continued to give me His Word of promise. He always reminded me of His commitment to sustain and help me, and not to leave nor forsake me. He told me that He is my light and salvation; I do not need to be afraid of man or anything. He reminded me that it is His job to lay me in the green pastures as my Shepherd and to restore my soul while remaining still and knowing that He is God alone.

I have always known that His word does not return to Him void, and He gives me perfect peace during the storm. This was another experience to test my faith in God.

Reflection:
How many times have you had to face a tough situation at work while having to compromise who you are?

_____
_____
_____
_____
_____
_____

How did this contribute to your breakdown and stress level?

_____
_____
_____
_____
_____
_____
_____

"Purpose is a lifetime process not a one-time event."

Everything we go through leads us to our purpose in life. We have to connect the dots and learn that at the moment when we feel that things are chaotic, we only need to become still in order to obtain clarity from God.

CHAPTER 9
Facing the Odds

A colleague notified me about another position in another division of the company. I was interviewed and was consequently transferred. I no longer had to deal with the program manager and vice president. However, I had to deal with management. In time, word got around to my new manager about all that had transpired at the company. My current manager, and I got along well when she came on board. I, however, refused to compromise my work ethics once again and that created a way for her to begin using negative words against me. At one point she said I "lacked common sense." I documented everything and included it in the correspondence to the company's upper management. However, I was told as a minority that talking back at her for all the negativity against me was disrespectful.

My project manager was not reprimanded for telling me that I lacked common sense nor was she for framing me as "frustrated" when she could not understand me. Based on my filed complaints against the organization, the upper management encouraged she to set me up, claiming that I was violating company policies. She terminated my position, and on the day of termination, she called me to apologize. I did not accept her apology but happily had packed up their equipment as I had just about had it. You see, a native tribe found this company with sovereign immunity for everything.

The organization can get away with everything. It was their word against mine. They had violated many government policies, and I refused to compromise my work ethics or who I am to support them breaking rules and regulations.

The program manager, vice president, and project manager wanted me to lie to clients and cover-up, but I would not do it. I would not compromise myself to support what was wrong. This was an organization that helped and promoted the program manager who left me nearly disabled.

The project manager knew that I was on leave through the Federal Medical Leave Act (FMLA) but decided to agree to frame me, which was the only way for them to terminate my position, claiming that I had violated company policies and insisting that my performance was poor. Yet she gave me a performance evaluation which stated that I was meeting company expectations.

Many of us say 'yes' to managers in order to keep our jobs, but in doing so compromise who God created us to be for a paycheck. I was not moved by the termination, as God had prepared me by moving me to start a real estate business. I initially took out some of my retirement funds and began living on my income from real estate while putting some money back into the business. God will always prepare you if you learn to be attentive and obedient to His Will throughout your life!

The company tried to silence my voice by offering me $5,500 so that I would not share my experiences to help others, but I said 'no' to them. I was not going to sell my soul to those who took advantage of others (including myself) and abused them. I was not going to say 'yes' to an organization who violated regulations to put the lives of others at risk and compromise their data. I know who I am and I will not compromise my life, myself or my values especially after gaining an awareness of who I am and what it truly means to be free and whole.

Reflection:
Where have you found yourself and how have you compromised your values and being?

_____
_____
_____
_____
_____
_____

What did you learn about yourself and your faith through the process?

_____
_____
_____

How has compromising yourself or sabotaging your integrity led to you making the wrong turns in life?

As I look back now and reflect on all my experiences to date, I realize that it is so easy to lose track of who you are and fall into the wrong lines. You have to realize that without documenting and learning the lessons, you will keep repeating patterns, self-hate and sabotage. You will become your own enemy without gaining an awareness and understanding of the processes in your life and journey.

"The odds lead you to find your wings, fly and become stronger and wiser."

CHAPTER 10
The Marriage

I had no idea what relationships were meant to be, neither did I understand marriage from the perspective I have now. I was conditioned to believe in marriage as an institution but the truth is that marriage is not an institution. An institution is an example of where you go to learn how to pass or fail—you either graduate or you don't. However, there is no graduation in marriage—neither is there a pass nor fail.

"Marriage is meant to grow you not grade you. You grow to understand your partner and vice versa. You grow into each other. ***You grow to 'grow' each other.****"*

I found myself getting married (although I never had a wedding) in my late thirties without having a clue what it was all about. It was based on my desire to escape all my pain and to be in someone's arms while forgetting about all the stuff I had thrown underneath the rug. I had no idea I was going to find myself in a place of struggle—struggling with my identity, struggling to find my voice and to find my way.

We both had baggage. We both had no idea who we were. We were both carried away by infatuation and lust and thought it was all love. Love was so far away from us. I allowed my convoluted and unclear thoughts to lead me to making choices that would compromise my stance with God. I had a calling from a young age but I struggled with it. I wanted to fit in like everyone else. I wanted to be in a relationship to get away from the memories of my parents' woes and my painful past. I wanted someone to fill the void I had inside of me without realizing that I needed to do the work myself first.

My ex-husband is a very good man in his own way but we both came to bond due to the pain we carried. I remember after a few days of my arrival in New York, I spoke to my mother and said I think I had made a big mistake. I realized I was not ready for marriage. I realized that I had made a poor choice again but she told me it was too early to jump into conclusions.

I faked being happy for a while but those around me could tell things were not going great. I would cry and pray. I remember, a friend of mine met my ex-husband for the first time and called me aside to tell me that I had settled and noticed I was unhappy. I held on; deep inside of me I was longing to be somewhere else, but could not tell anyone. My major struggle was with my faith. I would sometimes give in and ignore the Spirit and voice of God within.

> *"The truth is that when you die to the connection between your conscience and spirit of God within, you have died to yourself."*

It is like watching a garden (the very place where everything began after God had placed Adam in the Garden of Eden). You have to plant a seed. The seed either grows or dies. The seed will grow if you keep watering and nourishing it. It will die if you don't. The same happens in a marriage. You water and nourish your partner (and vice versa). However, you cannot nurture what you do not know how to handle or take care of.

We both had childhood pain that we brought in, and because of the levels of pain and lack of understanding of what marriage really is, we could not keep up. There was also my mother-in-law who spoke death into the marriage. She constantly told me why I was not the wife for her son. The abuse from her, was beyond what I could comprehend.

Let me encourage you, if a man's mother does not like you, and your husband is in a tight situation about who to support, you may find yourself in the middle of the ocean, trying to swim and stay afloat. I have healed and moved on, so I will not re-awaken any past pain. However, I have prayed and continue to pray for forgiveness on behalf of my ex-mother-in-law. I pray for my ex-husband daily. We have a child, and as long as I want the best for my son, I will continue to be friends with his father as long as God grants me life so that we can continue to raise our child, who's our God-given assignment.

What I learned mostly from my marriage, was the process of finding myself and setting boundaries. I learned to depend on God and trust Him more than anything or anyone. I learned that going after what you want rather than what God knows you need and has prepared for you, will derail you from your life's purpose. I felt there was a yearning and longing within me for something bigger. I felt caged. I felt the need for a calling that was beyond me but I never really understood it until I found myself.

I was in the middle of my master's program at the University of Maryland Baltimore County, UMBC. I was struggling to keep myself together and finish college. We had back-to-back conflicts that were not resolved but kept resurfacing.

I had a dream that pushed me out and made me really think about leaving my matrimonial home. I had the same dream three times. It was an occultic dream of me being sacrificed to save my ex mother-in-law's life. I would wake up sweating and feeling that my throat was gagged, and I would begin to pray. I could not hold down food or water and struggled to keep my head above the waters while going to work. One morning, my manager called me at work and told me I looked like a ghost. She advised that I start working from home until I became healthier. I worked from home and continued to struggle to keep my head above the waters.

I was mentoring women in church during this time. None of them knew what I was going through at home. One of them visited the house and as I saw her off, she screamed, "*Run...run for your dear life!*" I pretended as if I did not know what she was talking about. She asked that we go for a drive. As we drove down the street, I began to cry as she spoke to me about what she witnessed in my house. She called the Women's Crisis Center and handed me the phone. I thought it was someone I knew on the phone. The woman on the phone asked if I wanted her to send the cops and I said no. I promised her that I would report to the Center and seek help.

I began to be coached and planned to leave the house within a week or two. I was trying to avoid the cops coming to the house. I wanted my ex-husband to keep his job and not to lose anything. I had to see him through God's eyes. What would God do if He was in my shoes? Forgive. God will forgive him.

The following week was the third and last time I had the occultic dream. At that point, I knew I had to leave. I knew I had to stay alive for my son. I knew the season I was in was over. My ex-husband could not see or understand what was happening. However, he kept supporting his mother no matter what I tried to say to him. It was a battle between the spiritual and the physical and I knew I had to stay strong and remain on the spiritual side. God was not going to give me more than I could handle.

I asked God to take me out and I challenged Him: If He was still the same God that has been with me, He had to prove Himself again. I told God to reveal my life's calling to me and make a way for me if He was truly taking me out. I sat down and wrote a letter to my son, explaining the situation and letting him know that I was never going to abandon him. I had to leave the house so that I could stay alive and remain sane.

I began jotting down every detail of events that were happening daily. As I was struggling to keep myself together, mentally and physically, I was also struggling to keep up with work so that I could keep money coming in.

During this time, I was also having conversations with a childhood friend who I was trying to help. I had always known that he was gay but did not say a word about it (I did not want to judge his journey; I already had enough in my hands to deal with). He had just duped me while lying to everyone about our friendship. I got a call from my brother's friend asking me who this guy was. I immediately asked him if the guy had mentioned that he was gay. I had contacted his family to let him know that I was trying to help him while I was trying to set up a business for party/wedding favors.

I needed to make money so that I could continue to having an income. I had dabbled into making perfumes and since he had mentioned he had event planning experience, I thought it would be best to get him involved, since Nigeria had a market for the product.

I later realized this was a distraction and I needed to regroup and stay focused. I told myself that all I lost was money. I still had my life so I had to move on and let God continue to redirect my path. It was at this point that my family turned their backs on me but I was reminded by God of the story of Joseph. Friends and family members came up with different stories. Some family members and friends accused me of one thing or another. Some of my friends and family members did not know what I had been through or was going through. A few friends knew but never said a word about the situation.

"In the nick of time when life happens, you will realize just who truly loves you and will always support you through life's journey."

My oldest brother found out about the gay friend who had just duped me and thought I was trying to be in a relationship with my gay friend. I did not talk to my family about my perfume business. I did not want family to run my business for me as I had previously had negative encounters with them. I had invested money into it and offered to help a friend without knowing I was setting myself up for failure.

My family wanted me to remain in the marriage but I did not want to stay in an abusive environment any longer. They gave me an ultimatum to stay or they walk away. I chose to walk out of the marriage. I needed to stay alive and stay sane for my son's sake as well as for myself. I was tired of feeling caged and locked up. They did not believe in divorce; neither do I, but they also did not have a clue or understand what I was going through. I tried explaining but they could not understand it. The mentality in my culture was that if a woman left her marital home, she would become promiscuous, but that was not me and will never be me. My family became very spiteful when I needed them most. However, I was determined to find myself and get back on track with living truthfully and purposefully. I was committed to living the life handed to me by God (to find and fulfill my destiny here on earth) not the one where I was conforming to cultural, traditional or societal norms.

Some of those I thought were my friends also came up with rumors about me. The thought of a relationship was the least on my mind. I was trying to stay alive and financially secure as I was acquiring medical bills at the same time I was recovering.

I realized that people will always create a scene to mock you, break you or to control you. It was time for them to come up with the '*I told you so*' stories. Those who are never happy for you will show up and create a scene but I had to block out all the noise. I told myself the distractions were not what I needed. I needed to get on with God's plan for my life. I was tired of living a lie. I was tired of being controlled. I was tired of all the chaos. I was ready to break free from what was breaking me.

People will not always love you or be kind to you: Love them ALWAYS. People will always have something good or bad to say about you: SPEAK LIFE to them ALWAYS. If you only learn to treat people how they treat you, you will not have the time to show them God's love and grace that you receive daily. Always remember, their behavior has nothing to do with you. You should NEVER let anyone's attitude or behavior change who God created you to be and who you are.

I did not let anyone's perception cloud my reality. I knew who I was, who I was becoming, and understood what I was going through. Most of the time, we allow others to dictate how we live our lives and derail us from the course. I was no longer going to lead my life in the way that others wanted me to. I was on the path to healing and finding myself. I was focused, and it was at the point I began to write affirmations to help me stay positive. I wrote the following affirmation:

> *"No one can contain my spirit. I will own my truth and let it set me free. I will rely on God as my sole source of life. I will no longer become conditioned by the way others want me to go but I will stand and strive as I allow God to lead and direct my path."*

I was tired of using gifts to solve problems. It is not about the gifts he/she gives to you but how you weave into each other's lives and grow together that matters most. It was not about the emotional manipulation or control but realizing that if both parties are not growing together, you will only grow apart and there will be no love in it!

A marriage or relationship is not about looking to create a fantasy or to fulfill a selfish need but about building on a vision and creating a beautiful space and world for each other. It must always come from a pure heart. If there are games in it, they will someday expire and someone will end up getting hurt.

Reflection:
What is your understanding of marriage?

_____
_____
_____
_____
_____
_____

How has your past or pain affected your marriage (if you are divorced)? How is your past or pain showing up in your marriage?

_____
_____
_____
_____
_____
_____

Have you lost yourself or grown in the process?

_____
_____
_____
_____
_____
_____

CHAPTER 11

Purpose is Greater Than Life

I did not want to go to the shelter because of my son—he was the only surviving child I had at this point (I had four back-to-back miscarriages at almost seven months each after my son's birth). I drove out not knowing where to find an apartment. I had called everywhere and none had a vacant unit to rent out until January (it was October and it was already getting cold). As I drove around, I could hear my spirit say "turn,2 as I approached an apartment complex. I turned into the apartment complex feeling distraught. I pulled up in front of the office and took a deep breath with tears flowing down my cheeks. I composed myself, wiped my tears and walked in to the office.

The property manager was having a conversation with a couple in her office and there were two other couples waiting in the reception area. I asked her to spare me some minutes of her time, as I needed to speak to her urgently. She and I walked outside the office and she asked me what my story was. I explained to her that I needed to find a place urgently in order to stay alive for my son's sake and needed to move out of my matrimonial home immediately.

She asked that I give her a few minutes. She said they had only one apartment and that the other people waiting in the room were interested in it. She walked me to the one-bedroom apartment and asked what I thought. I told her that I would take it. She mentioned that it would take up to forty-eight hours to run my credit but asked that I wait to see what she could do to assist me. After 25 minutes, she said I was good to go and handed me an application to fill out. I completed the application and she told me to check back in two days – to give them time to change the carpet and perform minor fixes. I collected the key and went back to my matrimonial home. The following Monday after having the occultic dream for the third time, I decided to move out.

I did not have a bed. I packed my clothes, shoes, and a few new household items that were in storage. I moved into the apartment and continued working from home. My first night in the apartment felt strange. I felt humbled and lost. I lay down on the carpet and wrapped myself up with a comforter and some blankets. I cried out to God, asking Him what He wanted from me and why He was taking me through this painful process.

I received phone calls from my family members accusing me of being with another man but they did not understand that I had asked God to strip me of anything that was outside of His Will for my life.

For the next six to eight months, I was in a battle with God. Daily I challenged Him to show Himself and prove to me that He did not bring me into the world to suffer. I had to disconnect from family and friends. I became tired of phone calls with false accusations/allegations. I stopped answering their calls. I began to try harder to stay focused on what God was going to do as I continued to challenge His existence and wanted to face my reality.

A childhood friend I had lost touch with after I had left Nigeria contacted me while I was struggling financially. I had prayed to God for a financial breakthrough and God had made a way for me to build some websites for this childhood friend who gave me some allowance. From that, I was able to get a bed, TV, and home phone. I also paid some of my medical bills and gradually began getting back on my feet.

Day after day, God began to pour out the painful memories and lessons along my journey. I began to journal the events and the lessons and through these experiences my books, "*Love, Sex, Lies and Reality*," "*Being Single: A State for the Fragile Heart*," "*Beyond the Pain*" and this book, "*On Becoming Restored*" were born. It was not about the painful processes, it was more of what I had learned: The experiences, the conditioning, the lies, the sex, the truth, the conflicts, the tragedies, and the reality.

"If you focus on the emotions and feelings, you will believe that you are broken, but if you focus on the lessons leading to finding your strength, you will realize that you are being prepared for the journey ahead through the processes you are experiencing."

I began to realize that life was so simple the way God deemed it. We are brought into a sinful world and as we begin to learn to find ourselves and experience life, we become conditioned, and our exploration and discovery processes come to a halt. We start to live according to cultural, societal and traditional norms. Those are truly fallacies and far away from God's reality for us. No! It is not about the other people in our lives. It is about what we are or were accepting and condoning. It is all about the choices we make, especially when our minds are convoluted with illusions, conflicts, and pain.

I began to realize how my emotions, fears and pain/trauma led to making irrational decisions that were coupled with advice from others (who may have been speaking from a place of pain or from where they were in life...not necessarily where I needed to be). I realized I never really tested any spirit (anyone) but welcomed all without questioning how they were related to my God-given purpose. I began to see how worrying was robbing me of peace, while allowing my emotions to drive me crazy (you can read more on emotions in my book, "*Beyond the Pain.*")

I began to write down every single thing God was bringing to my awareness and I continued to take slow steps towards healing. There were days when I would laugh; other days when I would cry, and yet still other days with sleepless nights and longing for more of God's revelation. I began to gain conscious awareness of who I was really born to be. I continued to allow God to shape and mold me daily. The more I allowed God, the more I was able to identify the distractions, trials, and tests that were coming my way.

Three days after moving into the apartment, I went looking for the property manager and I was told that she no longer worked there. I realized she had only been there for a short period as my purpose helper. I began to understand the people God was planting in my path as I continued to gain clarity about my journey and life.

Food for Thought/Reflection:
How often do we recognize the distractions that come our way? How often can you tell if someone is a test or if they are there to test your faith in God? How often do you compromise who you are for what you think you want—and not necessarily what you need—in life?

_____
_____
_____
_____
_____
_____

You see, you will not find me trashing anyone in my past any longer. They were all there for a reason and a season. I either compromised who God created me to be without recognizing the distractions, the tests, and the trials for what I wanted in the moment, or settled to fit in due to culture, peer pressure, or societal norm.

I was in the process of getting lost in the past and was now on the path to finding myself while learning from the painful experiences. Daily I am becoming better and no longer becoming bitter and resentful. I am now focused on finding my truth, owning the experiences, and utilizing the lessons learned.

I had to own every bit of my journey...the lust, the sex, the lies, the façade, and the reality of it all. I never thought that I would have to walk away from my matrimonial home. I tried fighting for it but I had to make a choice to remain alive and live to fulfill my purpose.

"Life is a gift from God but what matters most are the lessons we learn from the people we meet along the journey, what life brings and teaches, and how we choose to live this life. Some will hurt, some will cheat. Some will steal, some will teach. Some will use, some will watch. Some will help, some will heal. It is, however, left to you to live life and not let life live you. You have to learn, love, live, and laugh through the journey. Always remember, you only have one chance at it!"

CHAPTER 12

The Separation Anxiety Phase

With my marriage coming to an end, the pain I had long carried within from when I was raped at the age of 17 began to flood my mind. The pain of rejection and brokenness all began to flow back like a stream. I had struggled prior to my marriage ending and now I found myself struggling to detach.

We have been conditioned to become attached right from birth. From a mother holding and nursing you, to fostering a desire to be held and cuddled. We experience the separation anxiety phase first as a child, and as we grow older, the desire to become attached becomes more evident. We become attached to friends, family, and others, and we have been made to believe that this is what love looks like.

In terms of a relationship, it is the longing and yearning we experience. We believe we need someone to make us complete. Hence, we must be in a relationship with the opposite sex to feel complete. Our emotions have become awakened (I have written in detail about emotions in my book, "*Beyond the Pain*") and the feeling of attachment takes a grip once again. The fear and illusions we may have created during our lonely days intensify the desire for attachment while longing for a partner. This often leads to us believing that this partner will make us become complete.

The moment the relationship ends, the fear and illusions are once again awakened by your ego. You have become obsessive, enslaved, and possessive of your partner based on the level of attachment. That is why it becomes hard to let go. This again is the basis of trauma bonding.

This was what I had struggled with for 15 years, even when I knew the relationship was not what I needed. I convinced myself to hold on, since I was attached due to the trauma bond with my son's father. This was the source of my unhappiness; the attachment was coupled with all the pain I had buried on the inside. This is the conditioning we have been raised with. This is the source of our limited beliefs and the enslavement of our minds.

"No one enslaves you, only your limited beliefs and conditioned mindset. This is why the conditioned mind can never be free of pain."

The attachment was more to satisfy my fleshly desires than my spiritual needs...my longing to fill a void the worldly way. The more I satisfied my flesh, the more my spirit suffered and my soul wandered.

Insight:
How has attachment robbed you of becoming free? What did you learn about becoming attached to someone without knowing who God created you to be?

_____
_____
_____
_____
_____
_____

Attachment and co-dependency will make you place your security in people and things. I struggled with detaching. I tried to numb myself by shopping and this was my way of pacifying myself. I did not realize that being attached and co-dependent led to so many of my insecurities oozing out to the surface. These have become the cultural, traditional and societal norm. This is the reason why it is so easy to be a follower and conform to worldly standards than become a standout you were created to be so. Separation from the attachment and becoming independent, became a struggle as I began to unlearn and learn while trying to detach.

As I continued to emerge into the new me, I struggled with letting go of things I was used to doing. The societal norm, the friendships and life itself. Some days, I would wake up and take a stand not to turn back. Other days I struggled, feeling different and looking like an outcast. The more I tried to fit in, the more I heard God's voice loud and clear.

The more I began to draw closer to God, the more the distractions showed up to derail me. I struggled and pushed harder to remain focused. I told myself I was not going back to fall for lust or satisfy my flesh. Distractions came from ex-boyfriends and friends from the past. I fought hard to shove them off. As I continued to stay focused, I realized all I had and needed in that moment was God.

The winter nights were challenging, especially when it was extremely cold. I thought about going back to the old life of being married but I told myself I was not going to return, especially after several conversations that did not seem to look positive with my ex-husband. Living in an apartment was so different from living in a home. I would listen to my neighbors making love at night and screaming, "Say my name." I had crazy thoughts running through my head some nights. I had to remind myself that promiscuity was not an option for me. It had never been and would never be.

Part of me wanted to go and party, using it as a means to numb myself (emotional numbness) to the pain I was experiencing. Part of me wanted to start going out to clubs and hanging out at bars but I was never that type of girl. I would hear my fears and my ego so loud, wanting me to be out there as a form of revenge. At the same time, I heard the voice of God whisper, "Vengeance is mine."

I cannot count the number of sleepless nights I had crying until I no longer had tears to shed. There were days when I asked God to take my life and let the pain end. I told Him I was tired of suffering and struggling between fitting in and standing out. I was tired of the phone calls from

ON BECOMING RESTORED

friends and family members not understanding that I was seeking God's will for my life and nothing else.

Winter after winter, I was longing to be held and cuddled at night. I was longing for a partner to hold. After a while, I trained my mind to seek more of God and less for my flesh. I eventually got tired of struggling with longing for companionship, cuddles, and hugs. I reminded myself often as I continued to write the books, that the lessons I learned were never to be repeated.

I also struggled with getting rid of the ultrasound pictures from my miscarriages. I would look at them and ask God why He had not allowed me to give birth, but lose the pregnancies. I would sit and talk to God like I was conversing with a friend. I thought maybe if I had the children, my marriage would not have ended but that was one the greatest lies I told myself. God knew if I had given birth, I would not have been able to cater for them, so He did not let things happen (He does not give us more than we can handle).

"You will never know you were born original if you keep choosing to live in the shadow of those you surround yourself with."

I struggled with hanging around fake friends who were only there to keep me at their levels. I struggled with saying 'no' to them sometimes but I was constantly brought to the awareness of why I needed to say 'yes' to myself, and love myself deeply while setting boundaries.

It was hard to watch myself back out of these people's lives after so many years but then, I had to remind myself that without breaking free, I will never be free to be the true essence God created me to be. It was not about the friendship so much, it was about finding myself so that I could keep a circle of people who were ready, committed, and living in their God-given purposes. Without that, I would easily be drawn into the drama and distractions that existed. I was tired of compromising who God created me to be who others wanted me to become.

The days I had my son with me, I would cry more as I watched him. I never wanted him to have the same experience I went through as a child but here I was, watching him go through the separation and divorce. I would speak to him and ask questions about how he felt. Sometimes I could see the pain in his eyes and I had to be truthful to him while helping him to understand that I had to be where I was in order to look after him while staying alive to be his mother.

I constantly spoke to him about God's will being greater than our will. He would speak life to me daily and encouraged me. My son gave me strength sometimes when I was weak; he still does to this day.

I told him I was never going to disappoint him as long as God gave me life. I reminded him of how much I love him and how much I was fighting to stay alive. At that time, I was going through several medical examinations to determine how I had lost five pints of blood. I was also transporting myself to and from clinics to undergo blood and iron transfusions.

I began to numb the negative thoughts by listening to praise and worship songs with my head phones on until I fell asleep. I would sometimes have a glass of champagne and go to bed right afterwards. I was ready to be committed to myself. I was tired of compromising the security that God had granted me from the day He created me, with the insecurities that society, culture, and tradition were setting up to scare me and put me in a place of fear, guilt, and shame. I realized I do not need to compromise who God created me to be. I realized that giving in to what was deemed normal was costing me so much pain and taking me away from my reality—the life that God deemed for me from the inception.

Most insecurities are born of the pain we carry and what the society shapes us to become, rather than who we are created to be. Fear begins to kick in and you ooze out your insecurities in a relationship based on the conditioning. Insecurities are one of the greatest sources of unhealthy relationships. They block us from receiving our blessings and begin to seek security in others. We begin to succumb to the way others want us to live rather than the way God destined us to be.

"Never place your security in people or in vain things. God has already made you secure from the inception. You only lose that security when you compromise who God created you to be with who the world wants you to become."

The insecurities I was experiencing were based on me being dependent on someone, with the expectations that all the pain I had experienced was going to disappear now that I was married. My insecurities stemmed from the fears and all the negative thoughts as well as my mindset. They allowed me to set unrealistic expectations. They led to negative decision making that resulted in negative consequences. Expectations are a set up for failure. Expectations are the source of disappointments, and disappointments are life's teacher, awakening you to a conscious level of your true essence. Why expect someone who did not create you, to take away your past pain? Why turn to man rather than turning to God? Man can never do what God can do for you: Heal, forgive, shape, mold or make you become the real you, created from the very beginning!

Reflection:
How have your insecurities affected your choices and decision making?

_____
_____
_____
_____
_____
_____

What expectations did you have that were not met, and what did you learn from each experience?

_____
_____
_____

_____

_____

_____

_____

I began to allow God to take away everything that was leading to me becoming more insecure with myself. I had lost a bit of my self-esteem and I had to learn to gain that back by believing in myself. I began to let God lead and guide me more than man did. I used to panic about things not being perfect, but as God began to do new work through me, I realized that only He was perfect, and that I could never attain perfection. However, I could work towards become more obedient to His voice, His calling, His leading and guidance while I humbled myself and acknowledged Him in all my ways. This was the beginning of my journey to commitment and love. I would have to sacrifice my longings for God's best. My longings were based on what the world deemed as love but was actually the source of hurt/pain.

The more I fought to remain steady, the more I struggled with separation anxiety. The truth is that you will feel like you are lost in the separation anxiety stage. You will feel the urge to turn back from the Godly path to return to worldly ways. You will feel like a stranger to yourself but it is how you come to learn the true essence of your being. One of the things that will make you stay strong is the peace you experience from within. I cannot use words to describe it. Every time I was faced with the crossroads of going forward or turning back, I could feel God's peace calming the storm and letting me know I did not need to worry about a thing. All I needed was to trust God.

I have come to understand that life is a journey. You will have to lose some people along the way if you have the intentions of finding yourself. That is what life is all about: Finding yourself and living in/with purpose; you learn, you live and you love. There is no life or light in the past. The past is a dark place to reside in. Leave the past behind but hold on to the lessons learned. Utilize the lessons in the present and let them prepare you for a better and brighter future.

Like a baby who is anxious when separated from a parent, you will cry and want to go back but you have to examine yourself and the situation. Did you grow or lose yourself? Did you become better or bitter? Were you elevated or depleted? Did you trust God enough before getting into the wrong places?

Reflection:
What did you learn about yourself during the separation phase?

_____
_____
_____
_____
_____
_____

Were you able to identify the weaknesses that gave you away or the strengths you are developing as you begin over on your own?

_____
_____
_____
_____
_____
_____

Do you really know how difficult it is to trust God, especially when you are going through the storm?

_____
_____
_____
_____
_____
_____

CHAPTER 13

Dead but Alive?

Being dead to oneself is not something obvious. To be dead to yourself means you are completely disconnected from your true essence...you have become emotionally numb and disconnected from your soul. You no longer have connection with God the way it is meant to be. Your faith is now based on what you can see rather than the unknown. The anointing of God has departed but you may still be engaged in routine prayer. The light no longer shines and makes you stand out but you are trying to fit in with everyone else. The societal norm and syndrome begin to catch up with you. Being dead may be emotiona.ly, physical, mentally or spiritually. To be dead mentally and spiritually means you are unable to see the truth and the need to move into a season of growth. It is not something you are mentally aware of at the beginning.

I realized I was spiritually dead but mentally awake. I thought about all the possible strategies I could pull but then I would go back to pray and still hear my spirit speak the truth to awaken me. The truth is that we are so clouded by the societal norm that we cannot hear the Holy Spirit's voice within. It is not that loud voice that speaks to you but the subtle voice that lets you know that you should not make that move.

You see, the greatest victories are not the ones you fight with your tongue or words. The greatest victories lie in the power of your praise and ability to pull through the storms. I began to realize that praise could break chains when I could not pray. The more I felt empty, the more I raised my voice and cried to God, and He would birth a song in me. I began to feel a lift in my spirit. I would become worn out and eventually fall asleep. I was short of words, not knowing what to pray about. I felt aloof and could not think about anything but praises to God would elevate me in the darkest moments.

I realized that power of praise. This was my soul's refresher: Coming alive and letting God speak to my heart, and I worshipped Him. There is power in your praise when you cannot pray. There is power in a song when you lift your voice in praise. You can break down strongholds with your praise. Whenever you feel your world coming down, lift your voice and praise God through the storm. Let your praise be louder than your pain.

The more I began to awaken myself to the truth about the experiences that had broken me, the more I began to see that being alive is a privilege when you come to know the truth that sets you free. It was not about rushing the process, it was about learning to trust the process while patiently waiting on God for guidance and direction.

> *"Pain will make you try to figure it all out*
> *due to guilt and shame.*
> *Pain will make you become fearful and begin to lead a lie.*
> *Pain will awaken your ego and corrupt your mindset.*
> *Pain will let you connect with others who*
> *are holding on to their pain.*
> *Pain will lead to irrational thinking and allow you to live on*
> *emotions alone. Pain is attractive; it seeks attention and*
> *sometimes affection. Pain will make you quit*
> *and stop you from moving forward in life."*

If you cannot pace yourself, you will end up rushing and messing things up. Remember, you have to learn to crawl or walk before you learn to run and jump. Life happens in phases not races. You cannot keep allowing people to leave you in pieces or allow yourself to die to the truth. You have to become consciously awakened to who you are. You have to realize your worth and remember who God created you to be. That moment will surely come when you embrace yourself for who you truly are and finally see your worth.

This moment came for me. I realized that, like everyone else, I was just existing. I was like the bottle broken into pieces and I kept recycling the same thoughts that led to nowhere. The thoughts left me repeating patterns. The patterns became my lifestyle. It was all recycled; same old stuff. Nothing new was emerging. I was dead to life, and alive to exist but not to live. I did not realize it until I began to feel like I was caged. I felt tired and worn. I did not want to fight the power within that needed to be unleashed. It is the moment you become consciously awakened to life again. You connect deeply with your innermost spirit and realize that you were never living the best life that God intended for you.

You may have sold yourself short of the worth God placed on you. It is the 'prodigal journey.' It was time for me to pick myself back up and realize my worth! I was not giving myself permission to live, but to die to myself. I chose to live. I gave myself permission to live.

The moment you realize your worth, you pick up yourself and take your leave. You suddenly realize that loving yourself deeply will result in a change in the choices you make. You will never settle for less once you regain the freedom to be yourself again.

"Death—the symbol of love many cannot fathom. It is meant to awaken you to find yourself. It is a remembrance that you came into the world alone to fulfill a purpose (not to get lost in life)."

Are You Giving Yourself Permission to Live?

Through it all, I discovered I was not giving myself permission to live, but only to exist. I allowed other people to make decisions on my behalf because I did not value myself or realize who God had created me to be. I gave other people permission to hurt me and I accepted the hurt they brought along. I gave others permission to lie to me and about me. I also lied to myself while accepting the lies others brought along.

I gave other people including my family permission to make life-changing decisions for me by seeking their advice and I accepted what they brought along. I gave them permission to reject me and I accepted all the rejection they brought along.

The reality is that we give other people permission to do whatever they want in our lives because we do not know who we are or how powerful we are. We do not recognize who God created us to be and we depend on others to help us find ourselves rather than depending on God. We receive the hurt and pain because we do not know how to set the boundaries. We lack the knowledge or wisdom required to put an end to it before it can begin. We have not understood that we need to be accountable and responsible for our own lives and journey.

Everything you accepted was because you did not give yourself permission to know and understand who God created you to be. I gave someone permission to rape me when I did not listen to my intuition—the Spirit of God within me, telling me not to attend the party where I was raped. I gave myself permission to be hurt when I did not pay attention to the actions but allowed myself to be engrossed in lust and infatuation. I gave away the temple of God within me to be abused and used for man's gain rather than God's glory. I gave myself permission not to trust God and allowed others to inflict pain on me however it came.

Today, I ask you as you read this memoir, "What or who are you giving permission to run your show?" Are you trusting God and allowing Him to lead you even though it may not be at the pace you expected? Are you allowing man to derail you from the glory that you were created with and losing yourself in the process? We are what we allow and who we accept.

"Give yourself permission to live. Give yourself permission to breathe. Give yourself permission to love. Give yourself permission to heal. Give yourself permission to forgive. Give yourself permission to trust. Give yourself permission to let go of what you cannot control. Give yourself permission to release the pain. Give yourself permission to be happy. Give yourself permission to grow. No one can give you permission except you."

Giving yourself permission is a choice. Giving yourself, permission is the beginning of life.

I chose to give myself permission to live when I took a bold step involving faith in 2011. I did not know where I was going but I knew there was something bigger within me and I asked God to take charge while I moved to the back seat of the car. I challenged God to prove Himself to me if He was truly God and allowed Him to take me by the hand.

I felt short while not giving myself permission to be me. I had to wake up one day to realize that I needed to give myself permission to live. I gave myself permission to allow God to lead me. I allowed myself to see that purpose is truly greater than life. I allowed myself to receive the greatest love from God. I allowed myself to let my light shine, rather than continue to dim my own light. I allowed myself to develop into a butterfly. I allowed my broken to become beautiful when I allowed God to work on me. I emerged into my true essence. I am not fully there yet but I continue to allow God to break, shape, and mold me daily into who He created me to be.

Do not be your own blessing blocker by giving others permission to walk all over you. Do not be your own roadblock by allowing others tell you how to live the life they never gave to you. Do not put a stop sign in your own way of growth by refusing to get help and to receive the help God is sending your way. Do not be wise in your own eyes and remain foolish to the things that God wants to birth in you.

"It is in times when you are lonely with yourself, that you tend to seek someone to love you. In those lonely moments, you should seek for answers in your own heart as to the reason why you feel unloved: Such times are meant for finding the missing puzzle in your own life."

Reflection:
What is holding you back from giving yourself permission to live?

_____
_____
_____
_____
_____
_____

Are you able to identify some of the areas of your life you are dead to?

_____
_____
_____
_____
_____
_____

CHAPTER 14
The Commitment

As I began the journey of commitment to myself, I felt powerless. I did not know the power I had within as I relied on my own strength. I began to lean on God for everything—and I mean every single thing! I longed for the ultimate experience of God's transformation. I needed to hold on to Him for strength every minute of the journey.

You may never know the power of God within you until you have had the ultimate experience with God. Most of the time, we think we know who God is but when we face life's trial due to our own shift away from who He created us to be, we rely on man in preference to God.

I started to experience God after my separation. I had prayed for days asking God to help me understand what the yearning was within my soul (to become committed to myself and to God's will for my life). I was restless while going through marital challenges. Part of my journey to commitment was to wait on God while praying to Him, asking Him to prove Himself to me. I have always challenged God as a child and I realized that the more I challenged Him, the more He revealed Himself to me. God always shows up but are you showing up to hear and receive what God has to say to you—either directly or through others? I was ready to be committed to myself.

With barely any support at this point, I began to identify all the reasons I needed to be committed to myself, own my journey and live my life to the fullest. After all, it was not about anybody else but me. No one can make me become who I am destined to be if I do not own and take charge of my journey.

I used to think that commitment was based on the saying, *"My parents/grandparents made me the man or woman I am today."* I have come to realize that they made me into the woman they think I should be which was based on their own experiences, both good and bad. God created you and I to be the man or woman He destined you to become and no one can know you as much as you know yourself. Others may think you should be a certain personality but God created you to be your own unique person.

What makes it hard to see the need for commitment to oneself is our dependency on others while placing God on the backburner. We focus on what is before us. We create competition against one another while trying to mimic someone else's life. Focusing on competition will result in losing yourself. You will not find yourself or your voice in that stance. Until you find yourself and your purpose, you may only be living in your own shadow. Until you become committed to yourself, you will not fully know the man or woman you need to be/become.

Commitment to yourself is an act of love—the love that you were born with should make it easy for you to commit to yourself. Due to not loving myself enough, I was begging and chasing others, wishing that they would commit to me and figure out all the answers to my problems. However, you must understand that no one knows your problems better than you.

"Until you become deconditioned of all you are taught, you will not be fully committed to yourself."

As part of becoming committed to myself, I began to heal from all painful experiences. The healing process for me began with grieving and forgiveness. I had to forgive myself and those who had hurt me in order to begin the journey of finding myself. This process involved going back to Nigeria to search for Kay. I wanted to forgive him and release him from my life. I wanted to break the soul tie.

I travelled back to Nigeria; my family had no idea what had come to do. I decided on my second day there to go look for Kay. I stopped at his uncle's house and introduced myself to the guard. This was the only place I knew I could find him. The guard directed me to his office, and on getting there, I told the receptionist that I did not have an appointment. I explained to her that I had traveled over 4000 miles and it was very important that I saw Kay that day. I had to wait for over an hour as he was in a meeting.

After waiting for over an hour, Kay came out of his meeting and screamed my name. *"Kemi Sogunle. You have not changed. You are still so beautiful,"* he said. He leaned over to hug me and I stopped him by raising my hands up (the rape experience triggered the painful memories and fear in me whenever someone tried to touch me). I told him I needed to speak with him in private so he suggested we go next door to a restaurant where it was quiet.

I followed him without saying a word. As we sat down, my heart began to race, I become very nervous and I asked God to help me speak without getting angry. I explained the reason for my visit and I started to tell him that I had come to forgive him for raping me during my teenage years. He placed his palms on his face for a few minutes. I kept staring at him to see if he would say anything. He had a remorseful look on his face and kept quiet for a while. He then began to explain to me that as a teenager, he did stupid things based on peer pressure. He said his friends had challenged him to do certain things if he wanted to be a man. He said he did not mean to hurt me and apologized for not knowing the extent of how his actions had affected my life. He began to explain all he had dealt with painfully and how is life had spiraled for years.

I stopped him from digging into his story. I was not there for a pity party or to get emotional. I was there to free myself from the soul tie and burden I had carried for so long. I wanted to scream and yell at him but I could hear my spirit say to me, "What would God do? Forgive and let it go!" I sat quietly then I stood up and told him that I would like to pray for him. As I prayed for him, I began to cry within but I held myself together. I took deep breaths and after a few minutes, I began to feel light within (something was lifted). I felt free. I immediately told him I had to leave. He volunteered to drop me off at home but I told him not to worry. I took a cab back home and throughout the journey thought about what I had just done.

A part of me had wanted revenge, but after listening to his experiences, I realized that he had undergone his own painful experiences and that forgiveness was the best thing to do. This was part of my commitment to myself. I needed to forgive so that I could break free from that ordeal.

I also reached out to others who had hurt me during the dating phase of my journey. I had to forgive and release them. Those I could not reach; I wrote down everything I wanted to say to them. I read out loud what I had written down and finally burnt the documents to free my soul from the ties.

I realized that forgiving them was for me and it was to unburden the heaviness I had carried in my mind for so long. Holding on, either unconsciously or subconsciously, to pain had derailed my thought process and contributed significantly to the bad choices I had made. Pain will only allow you to create space for resentment, bitterness, anger, and more. I had to choose to become committed to myself for a lifetime by breaking free from the past.

Commitment to yourself is a lifetime process; you have to follow the process that will lead you to finding yourself and connecting with your purpose. Without being committed to yourself in all areas of your life, you will look for people to become committed to you, but what you really do is attract people who hurt you. This type of hurt is based on your feelings and where you are with yourself.

I realized that without commitment, I had taught others to how to hurt me when I chose to settle; saying yes to others while saying no to myself. I anticipated that they would help me become committed to myself but that only led me to create assumptions and unrealistic expectations. Hence, I was facing the disappointments that led to me feeling lost rather than loved. My ego was awakened to fight against defeat but it was also deceiving me and allowing me to create illusions in my mind. My mind was battling to find validations and it focused on blaming others when my expectations were not met.

Commitment also requires facing all the insecurities that may have developed to the environment one grew up in and the fears that have built up over the years due to the painful or traumatic experiences.

I began to understand what commitment truly means. At first, I thought I was losing myself but I later came to realize that I was finding myself.

Commitment is a choice. The more committed you are to yourself, the more you see beyond your flaws and insecurities, realizing that they are your sources of strength and light. I came to realize that others may have hurt my feelings and emotions but they had not hurt my soul. My soul was thirsty for freedom and truth. My soul was longing to heal.

You cannot heal from what you do not talk about or deal with. What you do not talk about or deal with however, can hold you back from moving forward. I began to talk about my rape and my painful past, and I discovered that the weight was gradually being shed. I was becoming free from what was breaking me. I was beginning to realize that temporary people in my life were no longer needed to be held on to.

"Sometimes, the people you may think you need in your life, are only there temporarily. They are just meant to be a sentence in the book of life, not a whole chapter. Learn to let go and give yourself permission to learn and become committed to yourself!"

I owed myself (and you, too, will discover that you owe yourself) the opportunity to:

Find the Truth: This is one of the most difficult decisions I had to make. I felt guilty, embarrassed, and did not want to think of digging deep. It is the stage of letting all the skeletons out of the closet. I had to admit that I failed myself by letting myself slip several times and fall, but I did not have to stay down there.

Start to Own My Truth: I had to start owning all the things that I had allowed and the people that I had entrusted into my life without trusting myself enough. I had to own the truth that I was needy and that my neediness had led me into looking for love in the wrong places. I had to own the truth that not knowing myself had led to me giving myself away instead of finding myself. I had to own the truth that I had fitted in rather than stood out. I had to own the truth that I had accepted less than I deserved.

Stand on My Truth: I had to stand on the truth that the loneliness in my heart as well as the goodness of my heart, had allowed me to give myself to those whom I thought cared about me and loved me deeply. I realized that it was mostly their empty words that had connected to the emptiness in my soul. That led to me becoming attracted to their emptiness and pain. I heard what I wanted to hear but not what I needed to hear and focus on. I stood on this truth that it was time to find myself and live in my truth. I stood on the truth that I had failed myself several times and now, I had to stand on the truth that gaining this awareness was acknowledging that God was granting me the opportunity to break free from what was breaking me. I am now learning to listen more and talk less so that I can continue to stand on the truth that will continue to set me free.

Evaluate/Re-evaluate My Needs/Requirements: I have had to and continue to evaluate and re-evaluate my needs/requirements. The neediness and loneliness of my soul allowed me to push my requirements to the back of the room and focus on soothing my emotions/feelings. The more I did this, the more I got angry with myself for giving myself away repeatedly. Moving forward, I am set on the path to never losing focus on my requirements but evaluating/re-evaluating them as I continue to grow and as my needs change. Others may see this as high maintenance but it is a true value of my own worth and commitment to myself.

Set Boundaries: The lack of boundaries invites disrespect of oneself. I did not know how to set boundaries. I did not realize that a man can read the loneliness of my soul. This did not make me define boundaries that could not be crossed. It allowed me to say 'yes' to others and 'no' to myself. Boundaries are also required for everyone in your life. We sometimes allow others to derail us while seeking for acceptance and validation. I allowed the opinions of others to drown me while not taking ownership of my journey and life. I would give in to please others while leaving myself behind. It led me to become co-dependent while trading away my freedom to be me.

"Every phase of your journey will require that you outgrow some people by saying 'yes' to yourself' and 'no' to them. If you are not outgrowing people in your journey, you are not growing."

Never Lie to Myself: One of the lies I told myself was that I could gradually make things work in a relationship. I thought that I could change my partner despite the fact that I had already recognized the red flags. I lied to myself that things would change over time. *"Yes, he may not want commitment now but gradually if I made him see who I am and what I am made of, things will change."* This is the lie that gives some of us relationship woes. I had to choose not to lie to myself about anything in life anymore.

It is not worth it! It is a waste of one's time and burning off energy in the wrong places. It is a derailment from living to existing with pain. It is based on the feelings that were created from the buried pain...the rejection, the neglect and the lack of love acquired earlier in one's childhood. It creates a trail into adulthood and eventually becomes a habit that turns into a lifestyle. Admitting that you lied to yourself, allows you to begin to take ownership of your life and journey towards healing.

I have learned a lot through my healing process (and continue to learn as healing is a lifetime process) as I examined all the make-believe stories that I had told myself—all that brought me to lose myself and gain pain rather than healing and wisdom.

Find My Purpose:

"Your purpose is bigger than life but you cannot find your purpose until you have become committed to yourself."

The moment I began to commit to myself, I started to find it very easy to love myself deeply. I began to understand that no one can love me as much as I would myself. Loving myself led to my understanding (on another level) of what it is to truly respect oneself. After re-evaluating my life, I was able to identify what I needed vs. what I did not need.

Not loving and trusting yourself enough will lead you to attract a partner who will not love, trust or respect you. You will come to realize that if there is no love in the relationship, there will be no respect or trust for each other. If you say you love someone, you cannot hide how much you truly care. If you do not have the love to give, you will not be ready to commit to yourself or your partner.

Commitment allows you to accept yourself for who you are created to be and to become. If you are waiting for others to accept you, you will never accept yourself for who God created you to be and to become. If you are waiting for others to appreciate you, you will not appreciate yourself. If you are waiting for others to care for you, you will not see the need to take care of yourself.

If you are waiting for others to celebrate you, you will not realize that you need to celebrate your life, journey and little wins.

If you are waiting for others for forgiveness, you will not learn how to forgive yourself. If you are waiting for others to love you, you will discover that you need to love yourself first.

If you are waiting for others to speak life to you, you will not have time to speak life to yourself.

If you are waiting for others to thank you, you will not realize that you need to thank yourself when you turn an obstacle into a stepping stone (this will boost your self-esteem).

You must understand that you came into the world alone but you meet people who will either enlighten or derail you. Not everyone is meant to be there for a lifetime. This is why you have to commit to learning about yourself daily.

There will be those who will condemn, curse, judge or speak the truth to you but you must stand in your own truth and celebrate the acceptance of the truth that enlightens you to change your life for the better daily.

CHAPTER 15

The Commitment Process

I began to honor the commitment process. I had become so humble during the process and I did not want to return to my old lifestyle. There would be no turning back.

I Started Each Day with Gratitude
Every morning I woke up, I began to appreciate more and more the opportunity God was granting me to embrace myself and I showed gratitude for the gift of living. Every day was a new beginning in which I could accept that I could change or control anything. I accepted that I had to find happiness with a grateful heart for the gift of beginning life over again.

I Committed to One New Thing
Each day I receive the opportunity of living, I become thankful and encourage myself to become better. Daily, I commit to living in my truth. Whenever I find myself slipping into the wrong places, I re-evaluate myself to see the void I may have created, and I commit to finding the

truth in the experience. I own that truth and I vow to find one new way of commitment to myself.

I Became Committed to the Truth
I began to commit to the truth that I will never be perfect. Hence, I need to stop seeking perfection but allow myself to think before I act and reason before I react. I should not judge or assume but learn the truth about the experience and ensure that I am not hurting others in the process of living life. I seek to forgive in truth and love. I commit to becoming better than I was the day before knowing that each day is meant for a new beginning. This is my truth!

"Learn the truth; never assume. Understand the plight; never judge. Put yourself in someone's shoes; never hurt. Think before you act; reason before you react."

I Became Committed to Healing Daily
Every day is an opportunity to heal from yesterday's bad experience. I began to commit to a daily healing process. Anything I leave unhealed will attract pain to my life. The time I need to heal is now but I have to be committed to healing from this moment on.

Time will heal your pain if you learn to connect with it than let it slip away. Always remember, you can never go back in time and time is life. Wisdom can never be attained by holding on to pain but from healing and learning to move **'Beyond the Pain.'**

If your level of anger or bitterness is not leading to a

change in your life or relationship, it is because your ego is dominating. Life is a journey to be walked and lived. Never take for granted any day God grants you to breathe. Things may not always turn out the way you planned, but allow God to marinate and connect you to His Master Plan. Only then can you truly begin to live a life of peace. Remember, you are only here for such a time as this.

I realized several things during my continued healing process. I had conversations with several people who had not healed while on my quest to find answers. I spoke to a friend who had lost a spouse, and another who was divorced, in order to gain awareness. Based on my conversations with these two people, I learned the following:

A man who has lost a loved partner through death, divorce, or separation or has previously struggled with childhood pain will have his ego broken. He will tend to fight internal battles and when he longs for a woman, he will look for one who reminds him of his past partner or past pain. He will find a way to get through to her to pacify his sexual desires as a soother to his pain and once he is done, he will move on. If he finds that woman good in bed, he may revisit her for a rematch. He however does not have emotional connections which makes it easy for him to walk away from her. If he does not revisit her for sex any longer, he will move on to the next woman.

You see, most men are comfortable in their own space before thinking of bringing a woman into their space ... a woman who they see as a good fit or as an object to be used. Some men do not care for commitment but seek companionship for the rest of their lives. Unfortunately, it may be hard for some of us women to recognize this especially those who are extremely emotional.

This opened my eyes to see how men view relationships, how they think, and what we women may not understand without gaining such knowledge.

Without commitment to yourself, you will fall a prey to such a man. Gaining this awareness has helped me to recognize such men as distractions. With continuous healing, I have developed zero tolerance for such men but bring to their awareness their need to heal. This is a commitment to my continuous healing process and journey, to help others gain an awareness of the grieving and healing process as a life and relationship coach.

Without being committed to healing, you cannot truly love yourself enough to see the need to love someone as you do yourself. You cannot see or treat others as you would yourself. You will become selfish and use others as pacifiers to your pain when you need to be comforted, but it is so much better when you heal and move *"Beyond the Pain."*

A great part of the commitment process is to allow yourself to grieve while healing. Grieving is important otherwise you will become buried in the pain and past and will tune out anything that reminds you of the pain.

No one taught me about the importance of grieving. Grieving allowed me to mourn and to seek solitude in God. It is a form of conscious awakening to reality. Whatever died within led me to resurrect to life through finding myself in God and God alone. It is a transition from death to life. It is the freedom from hurt and conscious awakening to reality. It served as an opportunity to become authentic and true to myself. It is the beginning of my journey and long-life walk with God—a return to my first love. It is part of moving "*Beyond the Pain*" into a better and brighter future. It is the path to unleashing the world within me that I am yet to discover.

"There is a world within you that you are yet to unleash when you have not found yourself. The moment you come into contact with your true essence and gain clarity there is no going back to the old, and you know your life will be forever changed for the better. The storm is over!"

The truth about who you are is always deeper and greater than the concept of the person you believe you are and present yourself as, which is often tainted by past painful experiences; a mirage of your reality. Do not spend time living in the falsehood created by your pain and past. Allow yourself to own the truth that you are on a journey of self-discovery and that all the hurt/pain you will experience or have experienced is just leading you to gaining the awareness and knowledge that you need to uncover the real you (your true essence), find your strength, and become wiser to live authentically.

This TRUTH is what you owe yourself so that you can BREAK FREE from what is breaking you. The truth will always set you free but the lies you tell yourself will make you run and self-sabotage. No one can come to own that truth until you CHOOSE to accept what is, let go of what is not and what you cannot control, and break free from all that has been breaking you down. This is how you will find your wings and begin to soar in life's journey of BECOMING WHOLE.

Reflection:
What are you willing to do in order to commit to yourself?

___

___

___

___

___

___

What commitment goals are you planning on setting for each area of your life?

___

___

___

___

___

___

CHAPTER 16
The Life Lessons

I have come to understand that without a vision, or without setting goals for your life, you will live at the expense of others and anything/everything thrown at you along your journey. I have come to understand the need for life and relationship goals.

One of the reasons we get into messy relationships and find ourselves lost in life is the fact that no one taught us how to set those goals and to create the vision at an early stage. I look back and realize that if I had been taught how to set clear and specific goals at an early age, I may not have ended up on the path I took. However, I have to say those paths have led to the greatest lessons that have led to my growth and to where I am now in my journey.

Here are my lessons for life!

Be a Partner with a Vision

"It is essential that you create a vision for your relationship and become a partner on a mission. Be a partner of your words. Be a partner filled with wisdom. Be a partner who builds up. Be a partner who loves to be loved."

I am still working on this phase of my journey. I have created a vision for my relationship (if it is God's will that I will be in a relationship going forward). I do not need to fulfill my fleshly desires for a relationship until marriage but I rely on God's grace to see me through as I continue to commit to myself daily. I plan to have the best of God's vision for my relationship. God always saves the best for last!

Be love, give love, and be willing to receive love

Life is short. True love is rare. Be willing to give love, and be open to receiving it. It will come in due time. I believe in Divine Timing. Yes, I want a partner who will love me while I do the same, until eternity. However, my life has to be in accordance with God's plans for me which is something I do not have control over.

It is not about who I have become. It is about who I am becoming and who I am created to be by God. The person I am becoming, allows you to see the reason why I need to grow. Focusing on who I was or who I have become, is a way of holding on to my past but my past has no hold on me except when I choose to hold on to it.

Love does not reside in the past, it will only bring me

pain. I am becoming 'love to be loved.' I must continue to give the love I wish to receive without expectations or allow my emotions to lead me on the wrong path. I must continue to become my true essence daily in order to attract true love, not the packaged one that leads to nowhere.

Ask yourself, 'Am I becoming my true essence daily?" The person you have become, allows you to awaken your ego and pump up with pride. This makes you stuck and focusing on 'doing bad all by yourself'. The best will only find you when you become the best (by becoming your true essence daily)—when you have learned to love yourself, give love without expecting anything in return, and you become the love you wish to receive.

If you are in a place of pain and have the desire to heal and find love again but you are not making any attempt to heal, you will not recognize true love when it shows up. You cannot comprehend it because it is something you are not familiar with in that moment. You are currently operating in a place of pain where love cannot co-exist. It will feel strange and very strong. It will be too much for you to handle. You will only become defensive, fearful, and you will quickly awaken your ego. Your ego will make you think you are protecting yourself while self-sabotaging, and you will push love away and become angry.

You may become irritated but it is something you truly long for. It is just that you are not in a place to receive it. Pain cannot help you recognize love in that moment. Not until you heal, will you fully understand that love came when you most needed it but you were not ready for it.

Deal with the Insecurities

Our insecurities sometimes allow us to feel overly confident but not to feel contempt for who we are, especially when one area of our lives dominates the other areas.

My confidence was based on how well I carried myself and how successful I was becoming career-wise, but I lacked enough confidence in the relationship area of my life. I had been broken through being naïve, kind and nice. I had to dig through the reasons why I was always trying to please partners. There I found that the rejection I had experienced made me lose confidence in myself when it came to relationships.

If the wheel of life is not balanced, you will lack confidence in some areas and the deficiency shows up when you least expect it to.

I discovered that I would get in a relationship and want the man to be there all the time. I wanted attention and constant affection due to the lack of it in my life but the partner would not be able to give me what I needed. The partner or myself, would only become overburdened and eventually the relationship would end in a breakup.

It was not until I started healing that I began to gain awareness of this truth. I had not realized why I was pushing love away. The deficiency of love in my life made me attracted to those who brought this awareness to my attention. I needed to break free from what was breaking me. I needed to fill my cup and balance my wheel of life, not just saturate one area of the wheel.

I am still discovering some of my insecurities and turning them into strengths as I continue to heal and gain awareness of who I truly am created to be.

This is an area most of us are afraid to take ownership of: To embrace this truth and to learn the lessons it brings. This is part of the commitment journey to becoming whole and free.

Reflection:
How often do you examine your insecurities and deal with them?

_____
_____
_____
_____
_____
_____

Are you able to embrace the truth when someone brings this knowledge to your awareness?

_____
_____
_____
_____
_____
_____

Learn the Lessons
Part of one's life and relationship goals should be learning the lessons from each experience and what they teach you about yourself. What I discovered along my journey was that I did not know myself enough and I allowed others to

help me discover those parts of my life that I needed to gain awareness about.

"The most important life lessons are learned during the process. Pay attention to the process."

My daily goal is to learn the lessons each day and the experience they bring. To become aware of those things I need to grasp and gain a deeper knowledge as well as understanding who I am becoming. I choose to let each lesson teach me to become truer to myself than ever before. It is all about paying attention and learning daily.

Let God Carry You

We sometimes forget that everything we need and will continue to need; God has already provided. We tend to lose focus and search for things that temporarily satisfy our wants but cannot quench the longing for the deep truth and understanding of God's Divine Plan for our lives. It is vital to focus on the process without disconnecting from the divine love and grace that grants you the strength to keep on the right track. Choose to seek truth, peace and love. Let God's grace be sufficient to carry you on this journey while you still have life and can breathe. Align your thoughts with His and let Him continue to lead you through a life of transformation. Only then can you extend that which you have received to others and create great relationships in pure love."

Do Not Play the Victim

I realized that the victim mentality was a way to avoid taking ownership of one's experiences. It was avoiding the truth and shifting blame to others for choices made and what was accepted through those choices.

Stop playing the victim. Stop accusing others of being responsible for your choices. You have to take back control of your life and realize that you can begin to make better choices once you find yourself. Every disappointment serves as a teacher to the great lessons of life. Own it...face it...embrace it...change it by changing your thoughts and changing your life. That's part of what this journey is about. No one can live it but you. However, without learning from the lessons, you will only keep repeating the same patterns and denying life for yourself. Always remember that you only live once. Once is enough, when you have learned to be true to yourself.

What usually leads to the victim mentality is that we have become conditioned to hold on to the feeling of entitlement, especially when we have experienced disappointments from painful experiences.

I felt entitled to many things, so the victim mentality initially played a part in my seeking for answers from the wrong people and in the wrong places. These people who brought me pain were supposed to provide me with the happiness I lacked, the love I did not have and was seeking for, yet time after time I was disappointed.

"Entitlement sets the pace for unrealistic expectations, and unrealistic expectations will only lead to disappointment. However, disappointment serves as life's teacher, helping you gain wisdom in order to become better, not remain bitter."

Entitlement and expectations awaken ego, and ego stimulates fear in the process. Hence, why these three Es (entitlement, expectations and ego) are the greatest enemies of the soul. They only allow us to self-hate and lose our esteem further.

One of the lessons I learned during my healing process is that brokenness is attractive and addictive. As a woman, you come across a man who is broken and has not done the healing work. You become attracted and give in to sex without realizing that sex is a drug for him to obtain temporary relief from his pain. It is an ego booster, and you as a woman will become the pain reliever or pacifier he uses. You are now attached, and your soul becomes tied so you keep seeking his attention and affection, but he may not be available or may even become controlling. He will gaslight, smear and ghost on you. He will only look for you when he needs the sex and you become entangled in that web which leaves you confused about your relationship.

You have to learn to let go of him and allow him to heal. I had to learn to let go as I discovered that I was tired of being in pain and feeling caged. It is a difficult choice but you have to choose to break free from brokenness to live a healthy and purposeful live. That is the commitment you owe yourself.

Never Allow Material Accomplishments to be Your Driver
I used to focus on all forms of materialism and allowed those to cloud my judgement. I used to think that those achievements mattered but they were not fulfilling to my soul. They served as a hype for a temporary period.

If our focus is only on material success, we will forget about our emotional, spiritual and mental breakthroughs—those that supply the power to life and allow us continue to thrive. Never forget that the mental, emotional, and spiritual victories keep us alive and allow us to fulfill the material victories. If the battle of the mind (emotional, mental, and spiritual) is lost, the road to other victories will never be found.

Always celebrate your emotional, mental, and spiritual breakthroughs and allow others to witness the true meaning of living.

What You Feed Your Thoughts Matters!
I began to focus on healthy and meaningful thoughts, not what the world wanted me to think. I allowed myself to align my thoughts with God's thoughts for me and I continue to practice this daily.

"What you feed to your mind will grow.
What grows in your mind dominates and leads your life."

It is not the people who influence you that change the course of your life. It is what you allow through your thoughts and curiosity that influences your mindset as well as your choices. As a result, you can either shift towards a conscious and positive lifestyle or deviate down a path of chaos and negative lifestyle; a complete shift from God's Divine Plan for your life.

You always have to remind yourself that it is not what you have been through but what you have overcome that will strengthen you. You will have memories that will forever remind you and push you forward so that you can continuously transform your life and mind.

Reflection:
What have you fed your mind that may have contributed to the derailment you are experiencing?

_____
_____
_____
_____
_____
_____

What are you currently feeding your mind that is convoluting your thought process and limiting your beliefs?

_____
_____
_____

___

___

___

___

Never Silence Your Own Voice
I silenced my own voice for so long while allowing guilt, shame, and fear to hold me in a space where I did not belong. I no longer allow or accept silencing my own voice. Daily I examine challenges and issues I face in my journey while and speaking boldly about them and getting support from my coaches.

Silence is the greatest form of self-abuse when you choose not to talk about or heal from your painful experiences. Brokenness is exposure to areas of your life that you are not consciously aware of. You cannot have a breakthrough until you have eliminated your limited beliefs. You cannot allow those beliefs to hold you silent while robbing yourself of living the life God deemed for you.

Everyone Cannot Come with You
I realized that God places people in our paths for a season and a reason but not everyone can come with you on your journey. Daily examine the people in my life and set boundaries as needed. I let people off the bus when the time arrives and determine those that can come on the bus ride as well.

Not everyone deserves to be in your life. You have to determine who is worth going on the journey of growth with you. Not everyone deserves to be in a relationship with you. You have to know who is worth spending the rest of your life with. Stop allowing someone who does not deserve to be in your space to harvest your farm. If you allow everyone to pluck the fruits on your tree, there will be nothing left for you to harvest.

Learn to Be Happy on Your Own
Pain robs us of happiness. I realized as I healed and as I continue to discover myself, that my happiness will never be dependent on anyone or material wealth. I had to heal; to get rid of all hidden and known pain so that I could be free to be myself and to be happy.

Your happiness is not dependent on your marriage or relationship. If you are not discovering and loving yourself enough, you will never find true happiness in life.

"If you don't love yourself, you won't be happy with yourself. If you can't love yourself, you can't love anyone else. You can't give the love you do not have. You can't make anyone love you without loving yourself first."

Reflection:
What lessons have you learned from your journey so far?

_____

_____

_____

_____

_____
_____
_____
_____

How are those lessons serving you?

_____
_____
_____
_____
_____
_____

CHAPTER 17
What Lies Ahead

I do not know what lies ahead of me but I am choosing to live fully for every minute I am granted. I am learning the lessons and applying them, striving harder each day to be the best version of myself. I am learning to tune in daily to the spirit of God within me. I pray daily that God continues to teach me to discern and stay in His Divine Will. I am grateful for another opportunity at life to live and make a difference in the lives of others.

Looking back now, I discovered that I did not know how to discern early on or hear the spirit of God within me. I did not understand how quickly my habits became patterns and repeated cycles until I started to own my truth and learn the lessons.

"Watch your habits, they become patterns. Watch your patterns, they become repetition without learning the lessons. Watch out for repetition, it becomes a lifestyle without utilizing the lessons learned."

Repeated patterns will lead you to continue to re-enact your past which is filled with a conditioned lifestyle, limited beliefs, and core values. Every time you re-enact your past, you are taking yourself back to the painful process and having a mind-shift towards a conditioned and negative lifestyle. The moment you shift to the past, you will attract what looks like your past.

Every time you focus on the lessons learned; you are reminding yourself of why you should not repeat patterns.

I have since my healing (and I am still healing), grown to know and understand the woman that God created me to be. I am still on the journey of discovery. Life itself is a journey of self-discovery and it is filled with processes that we come to discover as long as we allow ourselves to connect with each one, and emerge.

There will be days when you feel that you do not want to go on and cannot seem to find a reason why you are still here. It may seem that everyone you turn to is letting you down and you just cannot seem to figure anything out why things are happening and why it has to be you.

I know exactly how that feels. I have been down that road before and sometimes still do. The truth is you cannot choose to give up if God is still giving you the breath and gift of life. People may give you reasons why you should quit but remember that it is God who gives vision and life, and as long as He is still granting you the opportunity to live, you cannot give up.

I almost gave up years ago, when my world came crumbling down. If I had, I would not be here to tell my story, or have become who I am today, and be in a position to challenge you to keep going. Always remember that when you do not have the answers, you can turn to God in prayer. It is not how fast but how well, and I want to encourage you not to be distracted by what is going on around you, keeping your focus on your journey. You cannot give up as God is still granting you life. People may not believe in you, but as long as God does and awakens you each day to see the break of dawn, He still loves and believes in you. Persevere, breathe, regroup, and remain focused while keeping the faith.

I have learned to become the love that I was created with and that I was previously seeking in others. I have learned and continue to love myself deeply; I have discovered the love that God gave to me from the very beginning. I am becoming more of this love on a daily basis.

I have come to truly understand what love is. Love is powerful and has no ending.

Why True Love is Hard to Comprehend

True love is important in every individual life but modernization has allowed the definition of it to be misconstrued with infatuation and lust.

To full comprehend true love, you have to understand who you are and know the love that resides in you as a person. True love is mutual. It involves two people who know, understand and have found themselves (their true essence).

"True love is not clingy, needy and does not seek for fulfillment...it is already fulfilled."

The main reason most of us cannot comprehend true love is because we are incomplete and have not found ourselves. Our souls are lost and wondering. We are seeking for others to make us complete but fail to realize that without being whole, we will cling to those who are out of our control while searching for true love.

True love is not clinging, lustful or infatuated. Those attributes are associated with romantic love which is of facial and physical value. Those will only take you through the 'honeymoon phase' which is based on feelings and emotions that expire with time. Romantic love is associated with anger, fear and pain. It is possessive, transactional and unethical.

To fully understand true love, you have to find yourself, know and understand who you are and understand your core values that make you live ethical within. True love is not focused or worried about losing the other person because it realizes the other partner is not in their control but is a gift from God...a person to share life and love with mutually.

You will be free to be yourself when love is true. It requires understanding the relationship you have with God first. As you know, you do not see God but the love He showers you with is unconditional. The gift of life and breath, the provisions for which you take care of yourself, the blessings ever so present in your life daily. The reason you give praises and show gratitude.

You have to understand that you are created in the image and likeness of God and as a reflection of Him, your partner will also be the same. You can look in the mirror and see yourself as one with your partner. There is no competition but collaboration. There is peace not chaos. There is communication and communion daily. You both grow and desire to see each other do better in life. You are not easily angered, you do not keep a record of wrongs, you speak and delight in the truth towards each other...no secrets; you persevere together...it is a union that is inseparable and selfless.

What we have been taught is romantic love that is selfish...seeking after gains, trying to control the other through manipulation, obsessiveness and possessiveness. Romantic love is a transaction and is stems out of fear while stealing your peace.

"Until you come to gain a conscious awareness of your true essence, true love will be hard to comprehend and experience. What you will focus on is romantic love and this will only lead to you living a life filled with lust, infatuation, transactions and pain."

You will base your decisions of feelings and temporary emotions rather than actions and reasoning. You will forget that feelings expire...when they do, you will end up repeating patterns which become a lifestyle.

Infatuation coupled with lust will always come to an end. Infatuation and lust will wear you out. You will get tired of trying to make infatuation and lust work for you the way you want. The truth is that they will both suck you dry and deplete you.

Love is a positive energy that pushes you toward compassion, kindness, trust, honesty, and faithfulness. Love is virtue. It allows you to see the reason why you and your partner cannot quit half way. It allows you to see that you cannot replace the partner God created for you with another rib. The rib God created for you or created you from, will only fit in the way God designed it. The true rib will neither be too small nor oversized; it will not come with conflict. It will not bruise you but complement you.

The struggle you face when trying to fit a wrong rib into a space where it does not belong will leave you with many wounds that are deep and take too long to heal. The true rib however, will support your healing process and lay down everything to make sure you are both fully knitted together as God planned it.

I realized that when I allowed my relationship with God to slip away, I found myself getting lost and building unhealthy relationships. If the first two relationships are not solid enough—the relationship with God and yourself—every other relationship will lead to you getting lost rather than finding yourself.

I realized I was searching for a partner from whom did not complement me...I was not the missing rib. I realized I was getting hurt, bruised, and depleted because I was trying to fit into a rib God never took me out from.

I have now fully surrendered to God's Will, part of which is to bask in His love for me. I have come to understand the need to be patient in love while allowing God to do the work in me as I do my part. I am no longer searching or seeking outside of God's will for me. This has helped and continues to help me on my journey to **becoming restored**.

Oh, what pure joy when you learn to know the truth that sets you free and allows you to see the light that you were created to be!

I found that my only source of strength was, is, and continues to be God. I realized that trying to find strength in a man was not what I needed. You have to learn to find your strength from within while relying on God alone. Always remember that if it is man-given, there will be a time when it will be taken away from you. Learn to trust God for all you need; He has already provided. Learn to tap into Him; let God pour His love on you daily as you drink from His well. Experience His Peace which no one else can give. Only then will you begin to live and come to appreciate each day He gives. Life is for the living—you only have once chance at it!

"Time is life, and life is time. You cannot take back the time you have lost but you can begin to change your life now that God is still granting you time."

It is very important to know and understand the season you are in at every phase of your journey. This will help you understand the processes you will go through, and it will help you to patiently sail through the wilderness and the stormy seasons. The storms may rage but the sun will surely shine again.

There will be the dry seasons (like winter), the blooming seasons (like spring), the scorching hot seasons (like the summer) and the shedding seasons (like fall). You will come to understand that each season is not meant to harm you but to shape and mold you while allowing you to emerge and become mature enough to handle the next phase of your journey. Each season may sometimes seem long but God will surely take you through each one if you rely solely on His strength rather than your own.

God has the power to help you overcome each season you are in. Trust Him completely and let Him lead you all the way!

Bottom Line
Everything we go through in life teaches us to find our truth and our voice.

"Light always reveals what is dark. Demotion always comes before elevation. Tests always come before testimonies. Trials always come before victories...a mess, before it becomes a message; secrets before revelations (you cannot heal from what you are hiding or keeping as a secret)."

They all happen to prune and strip us of all we know while moving us into who God originally created us to be. Do not resist the change. Embrace it as it comes. Recognize that without these experiences, there will be no transformation or growth. No lessons learned.

Learn to trust God, trust His process and align your faith with His will. Watch yourself grow from a seed into a tree with many branches of knowledge and wealth that you can pass on to others.

That is what life's journey is about: God's purpose for you.

"Although the branches may break off and the leaves may dry up, the roots are deep within God's foundation of love: The unshakable grounds. Therein lies your power to go and lead the way of love, light, and blessings."

Allow God's Love to restore you, knowing that love is indeed the greatest gift, and broken can become beautiful when you allow God to work on you.

I have come to realize that love is not about winning or losing but about healing and building. You cannot love anyone when you are in pain until you come to a place of healing, forgiveness, and becoming free. The more you learn to heal and love yourself, the easier it becomes to know how to love someone and build together.

"Love is better than life. Love is stronger than pride. Love is bigger when you learn to trust, become selfless and choose to speak life into one another."

There are endless possibilities when you give love without expecting anything in return. Always remember, life is a journey and no one owes you anything. Let everything you go through, teach, awaken, and enlighten you to find your way, seek the truth, and fulfill your purpose in life. As a seed planted not knowing if it will germinate and grow, so are we when we begin this journey called life.

We are meant to find our way, maneuver the difficult paths of the journey and come out better, stronger, and wiser so that we can pass on the knowledge and wisdom gained to the next generation. We must break down the walls and patterns that lead to generation curses. We must teach each child what true love is and how to live in his or her own truth. We must rise above the waters and learn to fly with the Heavenly Father's wings. Life is indeed beautiful. Love is all that matters.

"Your greatness cannot be found in a place of brokenness. Your greatness cannot be found in a place of hurt or pain. Your greatness cannot be found where you are not growing. If it takes a seed to push through the soil to become a plant, you can push yourself to make that shift, allow your broken pieces to become treasured gems and make you return to your place of greatness and strength."

As a woman I have come to realize that no man can know me as much I can know myself. A man may tell me what I want to hear but I have to remember that men are wired differently. I will only be running from myself if I allow a man's words to pacify me when I want to be comforted, rather than allowing myself to face the reality.

Don't let it be too long before you accept and embrace the truth. The truth doesn't hurt like you think. It only awakens what may be dead in you so you can begin to keep it real.

If I do not love you as I love myself, I would not have the

audacity to tell you as it is. Life is easy stop trying to complicate things. What you need is the truth balm to ease and forever take the pain away. Trust me, I know all about it...I have been there...done that and realized the truth is meant to free and heal me not make me bitter but better! I am still not there yet; I still struggle as I am human but I have to learn to kick the lies in the face to embrace the truth and make my journey easier!!

You cannot hit rock bottom —unless you take yourself there with your thoughts and worldly desires.

Understand that it is all about the seasons of life you go through. Allow each season to bring you teachings and blessings that will lead you to greater heights while you gain knowledge and wisdom.

Praise be to the God who comforts us in all our troubles, so that we can comfort those in trouble with the comfort we ourselves receive from God. The comfort I have received from God led me to become a certified life and relationship coach so that I can comfort those who are going through life and relationship issues. Not by my doing but through God's grace and mercy so that I can fulfill my purpose in life before I return home to Him.

"God has the power to determine the season you are in. Trust Him completely and let Him lead you all the way!"

It is my desire to find love again someday as I am becoming restored—**only if it is God's will for my life**. I believe in love and I believe in giving love to the one who deserves to have it in due time. I have become and continue to become the woman God intended me to be. I will never be afraid to share my weaknesses, low moments and true self to my rib when the time comes. This will allow him to recognize that I am never going to be perfect but I will be the imperfectly perfected woman for him.

   I strongly believe that love is greater than life and the more I embrace my true essence and live with purpose; love will show up at God's Divine Time. I continue to walk the journey of restoration and embrace the real me. *I am indeed becoming restored!*

BONUS CHAPTER 1
Some of my Quotes on Life and Relationship

1. You cannot calm a storm by steering it. You can learn from it by remaining still and letting the storm pass through. You only bury yourself in the storm when you steer it.

2. Make the Holy Spirit your best friend and you will never go wrong on life's journey.

3. Who accompanied you in your mother's womb? Who formed you and shaped you? Who grants you wisdom to continue in life's journey? If you cannot depend on God solely, you will depend on the world and lose yourself completely.

4. Life is not a competition. It is a journey that many people fail to understand. You have to work it with the vision and purpose God has given to you. If you often find yourself listening to the noise and looking at what is happening in the lives of others, you will end up going astray.

You will find yourself drowning in the ditch of worries, insecurities, bitterness, and resentment. Always remember, your purpose is unique to you and only you can fulfill it. Do not let yourself be blown by the winds of times. Only then can you fully come to the awareness and understanding of your calling. Do not focus on distractions, otherwise you will end up making round trips to nowhere and missing out on getting to the destination at the appointed time.

5. Sometimes we remain blind to our own ways, and until we come to realize who we are, our perspective on life may never change. The moment you come to recognize the love of God and allow Him to take away every blindness, dryness, and decay in your life, you will gain a new perspective. You regain your sight and your life will never be the same again.

6. You will sometimes feel like quitting, especially when things do not go as you planned—not as God planned. However, you must realize that quitting is a choice you make. It is choosing to fail yourself. It is choosing to give up on your life and purpose. Why give up when God is not giving up on you? Allow yourself to gain self-awareness in the things you do not know about yourself through the lessons you learn during life's journey.

"Self-awareness may seem tough but it often results in growth and significantly helps you to live the best God planned for you from the very beginning."

---

7. The greatest fear you have is the fear of being your true self. Why do you have the fear of being your true self, you may ask? Well, once you have awakened fear, ego comes in to delude you about your true essence. It creates a persona that you cannot seem to get over; an alteration of your true being, and you can only begin to live a lie onward at this point.

This is a choice you subconsciously make without knowing it. It is so easy to choose this option because of those you surround yourself with: Those who do not hold the same values as you; those who are not looking to improve on the quality of their lives but are ready to hold you back from living yours. You find yourself yielding to peer pressure and believe that life is a reflection of those who are 'in the know,' but the question is, "What do they really know?" If what they know does not help you advance in life, you will hold yourself back from living and join those who are existing.

8. There is no greater joy than discovering your own strengths through your weaknesses. It is all about finding your truth and living it out loud.

9. When you love someone, you see beyond their physical characteristics. You feel their energy; you connect with their true essence. You do not lust after them or become infatuated. You become one with their soul and see beyond their imperfections. That is when you can fully understand it was meant to be: God ordained and appreciates them as a gift and blessing in your life.

10. The moment you realize that your God-given vision is bigger than your current state, you begin to feel caged, and you know it is time to move to your next level. Sometimes you may need to be hurt in order to learn the lessons. This makes you strong. You realize that it is not about the battles but about getting 'Beyond the Pain,' looking back someday while laughing and saying to yourself, 'I know better now not to settle for less than I am worth.'

11. Difficult people come into your life to show you what you do not need, to make you learn more about yourself and to teach you how to set boundaries. Be sure to thank them and love them; do not hate or hurt them.

12. Ego is often awakened by fear (fear of rejection or of being alone), as a form of self-defense, often due to hidden pain. This leads to illusions in the thought process, thus making it easier to subconsciously hurt the one you love.

13. **Your life is a tree. What fruits are you bearing? Are you growing? Who is watering your roots? The more you find yourself (your true essence), the fewer people you will have in your life; the healthier and peaceful your life becomes.**

14. If God wanted you to be a copy, He would not have created you as an Original. If God wanted you to be a shadow, He will not have created you as a Light. Find yourself and be the best version of you that God created.

15. Don't expect a partner who has not discovered his/her wings to help you fly. Don't expect a partner who has not

found his/her voice to help you speak life. Don't put your life in the hands of others when you have not learned to live.

16. The moment you run away from your problems you begin to run into more problems rather than find solutions.

17. When you omit God and prayer from your life, you choose to omit peace from your life while inviting pain into it. The most painful decision you will have to make is that of self-discovery. However, you cannot choose to remain in a locked-up world of unconsciousness if you need to grow and emerge into a higher level of self.

18. Each day you wake up is an opportunity for a brand-new start. You have been granted life for a purpose but it is up to you to find your purpose in each day. You may not know what lies ahead but you must strive to see the possibilities each day holds. As the cloud shifts, you must shift and align yourself with every blessing and challenge that each day brings in order to live and fulfill your purpose.

19. It is in times when you are lonely with yourself that you seek someone to love you. In those lonely moments you should seek for answers in your own heart as to the reason why you feel unloved. Such times are meant for finding the missing piece of the puzzle in your own life.

20. You plant seeds and nurture them while watching as they grow. Learn from this; plant seeds of love and water them so that you can nurture your relationship and watch it continue to grow with time.

21. Don't feed your ego and starve your soul. Listen to your intuition and nourish your soul. One day you will look back and realize that the pain meant nothing without the lessons you were meant to learn in order to emerge into a higher level of who God created you to be and to embrace all the lessons you learned through the process. Everything was shaping you for this moment of growth, love, and wisdom to rise above it all!

22. God's intentional plan is never about your ways but about His purpose and will for your life. It is not about where you want to be but about where He needs you to be. Your earthly desires are never part of His intentional plan: the main reason why you are lost is because you took your focus off Him. Never let your focus shift from God's presence and purpose. You don't need to be lost. You need to find yourself in God but your plan will lead you to become lost and miss out on God's plan for you.

23. Ask yourself daily, how has your relationship helped you find yourself, and build a stronger relationship with God, or helped you connect to your God-given purpose?

24. Never allow a man or woman to take away the power that God has given to you. He created each woman as a helpmate for a man, not for multiple men. Stand in your truth; reclaim your crown and refuse to diminish yourself. Wait for your rib and let God bless you and him as you both grow together in love, not in lust and infatuation.

25. The process may cost you for a season but God is preparing you for a lifetime. Trust the journey and don't focus on what's behind.

26. We are created to see others as we see ourselves and treat others as we treat ourselves. The truth is, you cannot treat anyone with love when you do not fully understand what love really means.

27. Every choice you make comes with a consequence you face and no one will help you face those consequences. Choose to seek Godly wisdom and allow your spirit (intuition) guide you always. At the end of life, only you will give an account for your life. Choose to live and stop existing: Your choice; your reality. Many are lost but very few are found!

28. "Life may throw you curveballs but what you do with them is a decision you have to make. You can choose to become better, push harder and turn them into stepping stones towards your greatness or sit on them and allow them to make you bitter. The outcome of the choice you make will determine the course/path you take. Always remember that no one can walk in your shoes or fulfill your life's purpose. There's a reason why God chose and equipped you for it. He knows you can make it through as long as you stay focused and press in with Him by your side. A process is not a final destination but a preparation for the next phase in your journey. Never give up thinking you are not capable; you can do the impossible. Believe in yourself and know that you are unstoppable!"

29. "We live in times when lack of self-esteem/confidence and constant seeking for attention and validation is deemed as social proof. We live in a society that glorifies

lies as storytelling and those seeking help are being taken advantage of.

30. Faking it to make it has become societal norm and reality has been misinterpreted for fantasies and impersonation. The more you cannot tell anyone the truth, the more you will keep lying to yourself.

31. Not everyone who started your journey with you will finish with you. Some are meant for the beginning, some are passers-by, some who help you transition, some who will challenge you, and others who are meant to finish the process with you. Be prayerful and learn to discern who belongs where so you don't place the wrong people in the right path and the right people in the wrong path—you alone will suffer the consequences for doing so, it's your race not theirs. Be wise!

32. "Without any set goals or a vision for your life and for accomplishing things, you will become dependent on others and set unrealistic expectations that will never be met. You will become disappointed and resentful of others. Disappointments, however, teach you how to get back on track and become independent, ...realizing that no one can understand or give you what you are seeking without attempting to accomplish those yourself. Always remember, your life is your own race and the only one who can stop you from shinning your life and accomplishing your set goals is you."

33. Assumptions, unrealistic expectations, and neediness are signs that you are not fully healed, and that you don't feel complete, ready for a grown relationship.

34. Without exiting from your past experiences, there will be no new beginnings. Embrace the past lessons and prepare for what is coming.

35. "Ask yourself, "Is this the life I want to live? Do I believe I deserve better? What is stopping me from getting there?" If you don't believe it, you won't receive it and you cannot accomplish it.

36. Never regret life experiences. Every experience serves as a teacher, reminding you to find your true essence by looking deep within. It is always good to end a phase of your life and start over again. Each chapter you go through in life is going to be different. You cannot hold on to the last chapter if you want to move "Beyond the Pain."

37. You may sometimes feel that you have reached the end of the road, and life may seem to be taking its toll on you, but God still reminds us every fall that there is beauty in dead leaves. Find strength within and push through the storms. You are stronger than you think!

38. You may sometimes feel as though you are buried underneath the rubble, but God is actually hiding you from the things that will steer you away from Him. You may cry your last tears and ask Him to take your last breath, but then He reminds you that He's not done with you yet. Get this: It's the beginning of your breakthrough. No, you did not break down, it was a test of your faith so that you can remain strong and grow in God.

39. Your mind is your tool house. It is the most powerful weapon handed to you by God. You can either use it or lose it!

40. Every test and mess will result in your growth and lead to you learning life lessons. Never resist the mess and tests. They are meant to help you emerge into a higher level of yourself.

41. Never place your security in people or vain things. God has already made you secure from the inception. You only lose that security when you compromise who God created you to be with who the world wants you to become.

42. Forgiveness does not always come easy. You feel the pain and you inflict more pain on yourself when you hold on to the past rather than let it go. You only rob yourself of happiness and peace when you choose not to forgive and let go!

43. We would understand each other better if we took the time to figure out the lessons. We can learn from one another without trying to prove who is right or wrong. We can only learn to live in love, peace and harmony when we learn to let go of our ego and admit that no one knows it all. "To truly love yourself requires that you forget about everything you know and become humble. Only then can you truly gain deeper wisdom that only God can give!"

44. What seems like a breakdown always leads to your breakthrough.

45. We become conditioned by repeating patterns that become routine. Those routines become habits, and habits eventually may become addictions. The challenge is to strive hard and change so that you can unlearn and learn

while taking risks and while making choices that do not allow you to become stuck, or to become an addict of your own habits.

46. Happiness is not on sale. You cannot find it anywhere but within you. Stop searching for it anywhere but within you. Stop searching for it on the discount rack!

47. In times of adversity, the true meaning of family and friendships will be redefined. There will be the rumor mongers, the distractions, the onlookers, and those who stick with you through thick and thin. It is a season to separate the shrubs from the trees. Always remember that as you emerge into a higher level of self, 'Trees do not bend backwards to become shrubs but continue to grow upright.'

48. ***Love is FREEDOM to be yourself, to accept your flaws as the keys to finding your strength, to realize that experiences bring about the lessons which result in blessings."***

49. No one can make you fail unless you choose to accept failure as your only solution.

50. The end of a season will only lead you to the beginning of another one. If you choose to focus on the one that ended, you will never step into the one that is about to be birthed. Life is a journey of becoming and it allows you to become refreshed so that you can continue to grow and walk in your purpose.

51. "You learn to kick your fears goodbye. You learn to stand in your own voice. You learn to choose to become responsible and accountable for your life and journey. You

learn to say 'no' to anything/anyone that no longer serves you. Most of all, you learn to heal, forgive, be at peace, and live. You learn that existing is no longer an option. You learn to find yourself and get back on track. You learn to be grateful for each obstacle because you know each one is an opportunity, leading to your growth. Always remember that existence is easy but learning and growing are much more important to you in becoming better than remaining bitter."

52. "People who dwell on your past cannot help grow or overcome the past. They will only hold you in a place of pain and take you to the past. They cannot comprehend your growth or understand why you have outgrown them. Never give them an opportunity to take you to the past where you do not belong. The past has no hold over you and no longer exist."

53. "If your friends and family cannot support you to become a better and heathier version of yourself daily, you may be trauma bonding and surrounded by/with toxicity."

54. "Toxic partners are usually inconsistent. They may try to win you over by love bombing you. Always remember to focus on their actions rather than their words. It would not take long before their masks begin to fall off."

55. "Have faith and always believe in yourself. Love and trust yourself so that you can eliminate doubt and fear. Strive harder daily in your journey to becoming a better version of yourself. Most of all, pray daily and master patience along the way...you will surely gain clarity when you do."

56. I pray your soul finds peace and rest. I pray you heal and understand the power of forgiveness. I pray you experience the joy only God can give. I pray you know and experience love like never before. This is my daily prayer for you.

BONUS CHAPTER 2

Daily Affirmations

1. Today, I choose to accept my oneness with God.
I choose not to doubt His love for me.
I choose not to question His protection and care.
I choose to give Him my pain in exchange for His healing and peace. I choose to accept that I am, indeed, a miracle. I choose to trust Him completely and rest in His love for me.

2. I choose to see blessings in every situation. I choose to love at all times. I will not block my blessings with pain. I choose to learn from everything that happens to me. I choose to live in abundance and peace.

3. I will not hold on to anything valueless. I will not hold on to things I cannot change. I will move 'Beyond the Pain' into my purpose. I will accept God's plan for me and let go of mine. I will receive God's peace and find strength in Him alone. I will align my thoughts with God's thoughts. I will embrace God's love for my life for eternity.

4. Nobody can contain my spirit or impose a limitation on me that God did not create. I am who God made me to be and become. I will forever remain true to myself. I will be the light I was born to be. I will forever remain in Him.

5. I am as God created me. Light, peace, and joy are mine and will abide with me. I will see myself in this context alone. I am, indeed, a miracle.

6. I am not weak. I am strong. I am not helpless. I am powerful. I am not limited. I am unlimited. I am not doubtful. I am certain. I am not an illusion. I am the reality. I am not of the dark. I am of the light.

7. I am a miracle. I am God's chosen child and vessel. I will stand in the midst of the crucible. I am alive. I am possible and God will forever hold me in His light and love.

8. God's gifts to me today are joy and peace. No one else can offer me these gifts. These are precious gifts that entail no loss, only gain. God's gifts to me hold no limit. I will embrace my joy and peace.

9. I choose to center my thoughts on positive outcomes. I choose to see possibilities and not disappointments. I choose to see peace not chaos. I choose faith over fear. I receive, I believe and I will achieve!

10. I choose to accept my oneness with God. I will not doubt His love for me. I will not question His protection over me. I will give Him my pain in exchange for His peace. I am truly God's gift. I am indeed a miracle!

11. I choose to see blessings in every situation. I choose to love at all times. I will not block my blessings with pair. I choose to learn from everything that happens to me. I choose to live in abundance and peace.

12. No one can contain my spirit. I choose to hold on to it. I will not give myself away to be used or abused but will honor the temple of God that I am while standing up for the truth and in/with my own voice.

BONUS CHAPTER 3

My Thoughts on Life and Relationships

No one teaches us what relationship building is all about. You may grow up in a broken or healthy home but what you tend to do is mirror everything you see around you. You begin to imagine that your relationship will be like that of A or B (or even better).

The pain you carry from watching the fights, backlashes, and abuse tends to follow you in your relationship and lead to you repeating patterns. You find yourself in the wrong places while looking for love. You may even try to make it work, but nothing happens.

It will come to a point where you become tired. Tired of trying to make the other person see what you are seeing, of trying to change the other person or trying to figure it out on your own.

The truth is that you go in with a lot of assumptions and expectations but it does not take long before everything crumbles. The following are Major Reasons Why Relationships

Do Not Last:

Relationships require a lot of work but without focusing on the three major reasons why relationships end, you may think that your partner is the problem. Relationships end and divorce may happen without the awareness of these three things:

1. **Assumptions**: You assume that your partner will be a certain persona that you may have created but you do not know or understand your partner enough.

"Knowing someone on the surface is different from knowing someone in-depth. – 'Beyond the Pain' © 2014 Kemi Sogunle. All Rights Reserved."

---

2. **Unrealistic expectations** – You believe that your partner will meet your wants and be who you want them to be. You become disappointed when your expectations are not met and your relationship becomes sour. The ugliness in a partner is revealed due to unrealistic expectations during a divorce.

3. **You do not know, accept or value yourself enough** – Without knowing and understanding yourself, you cannot accept and value yourself enough. You have to understand that your weaknesses lead to your strengths, and that leads to you knowing and understanding yourself more. The more you know and understand yourself, the more you accept and value yourself.

Relationships will last longer if you take the time to

know and understand your partner without creating assumptions, setting unrealistic expectations, and getting to know and understand yourself, so that you can know and meet your own needs while waiting for /finding a partner who will complement you.

I have learned through this journey of self-discovery and conscious awakening that if you do not discover yourself, other people you meet while trying to build on a relationship will expose the things you need to know and learn from. We have been conditioned to see these exposures as hurt or pain rather than an awakening to self-evaluation.

I began to ask myself the following questions while learning to uncover my truth and find myself:

- How much do I know about myself?
- What am I yet to discover about who I am?
- What is the purpose of everyone I meet in life and on my journey?
- Who are my purpose helpers, pushers, stoppers, or killers (read more in my book, "*Being Single: A State for the Fragile Heart*")?
- What are those things I am choosing to accept that derail me from the course that God set before me?

These questions and others, led to defying moments that, in turn, led to my transformation. I am still emerging and on the journey of self-discovery. After all, that is what life is about: To find yourself, to live with the love you were born with while sharing it with others and to fulfill your purpose. Without finding yourself, you may never discover who God really created you to be.

It is so easy to seek answers in a partner, to want to get married for the wrong reasons, or because everyone else is getting married; to have someone else love you and take responsibility for your life. But without discovering your own wings, you may end up crashing and dying to yourself.

Never make assumptions based on your fears and struggles. Always make your intentions known and be free to speak your mind from the very beginning. Do not think that by expressing yourself, you will lose a partner.

You cannot lose a partner who God created and designed for you but you can attract distractions that mimic the real deal.

The moment you start to make assumptions, you will set unrealistic expectations and allow fear to dominate. You will try to control the situation and relationship in order to have your expectations met. However, when it does not happen, you feel drained and disappointment. This should always lead you to accept what is, to accept that you lied to yourself about making things work and now you have to own it and learn the lessons which are not to be repeated. This is a huge step in your growth and maturity.

Embracing this truth will lead to you learning more about yourself; realizing that you need to know your needs (not focus on wants): You need to define your territory and utilize your requirements in order to vet those you meet. This will prepare you for finding the right partner after you have come to understand yourself. It is all about establishing a solid foundation for the relationship with yourself and God first, which will set the pace for every relationship you encounter while here on Earth.

I had to come to terms by embracing my past and pain as part of my growth journey. I have realized that no matter what I go through, no one can help me heal or walk the journey that God set before me.

If a partner does not realize his or her own voice before you meet, he or she will only help you to drown, not to soar.

"Do not expect a partner who has not discovered his or her wings to help you fly. Do not expect a partner who has not found his or her voice to help you speak life. Do not put your life in the hands of someone who has not found himself/herself. Such a partner will only help you exist rather than live."

You will come to realize that the more you become who you are created to be, the less you will tolerate anything that is not in line with your God-given vision and purpose. Be it friendship or romance, you will determine who's worth keeping in your circle and who needs to go.

Your relationship will be unique when you do not allow worldly standards to define how you connect with your partner, how you shower each other with love, how you do the silly things that bring joy to your friendship/relationship and that allow you to grow together deeply. You will not have to set the pace based on what the world thinks love should be for both of you, you will define love in your own terms and live the best years together.

Life is short and meant to be lived, but if you choose to live in misery you will become sad, stuck, and lost in the process. You have to constantly evaluate your current status, and know when you need to pivot or realign yourself to stay on track. You will know when to let go and when to hold on; when to grieve and when to heal. You will come to understand what it means to be healthy and to live purposefully. Life is to be lived to the fullest and with purpose, but without knowing who you are and why you are here, you may end up becoming a wandering soul rather than emerging higher to become stronger and wiser, while living your best life.

ABOUT THE AUTHOR

Kemi Sogunle is a **certified professional life and relationship coach and expert,** award-winning international speaker, and multi-award-winning author of *"Love, Sex, Lies and Reality," "Being Single," "Beyond the Pain" and "On Becoming Restored."* She is listed as one of the best 10 coaches in Maryland, USA by Thumbtack.com (2015, 2016 and 2017).

She is also a life coach and relationship expert on selfgrowth, as well as a dating expert on Older Dating UK.

Kemi has been featured in Essence, Bravo, NBC News, NAACP, National Association of Adult Survivors of Child Abuse, International Newspapers, Redbook, Zoosk, and she is also contributor to The Huffington Post.

Mission:
Kemi's **purpose** in life is to **support single men and women who are ready to gain a conscious awareness of who they are** after a broken relationship or divorce, **to heal from their painful past experiences, to learn to love themselves,** and to develop **positive and healthier relationship habits.** She is **committed** to **helping singles and married couples gain a**

deeper understanding of their lives and relationship vision while **living truthfully and purposefully** to make their lives become **better not bitter.**

Her Story:

Kemi coaches, writes and speaks from a personal place as well as from **experience on abuse, relationships, healing, forgiveness, and purposeful living** by **moving from pain to purpose.** She began her journey to becoming a life and relationship coach after her separation and divorce, which led her to soul-searching. Raped at age 17, she kept this to herself and never healed from it. This led her to looking for love in the wrong places. After her painful divorce (after 15 years of marriage), she embarked on a journey to finding herself, and she connected to her spirituality while learning to view life from a different perspective. She found herself, healed, and gained a deep understanding of life and relationships as well as her purpose in life. She shares deep and inspirational messages through her writing and has touched many lives across the globe. She also teaches and inspires others to become the best version of the person God created them to be on daily basis. She believes that **living truthfully is paramount to long-lasting relationships and healthy living**.

She has also served as a volunteer with the Center for Pregnancy Choices and the American Red Cross Key Chapter, Meridian, MS. She enjoys spending time with her son, gardening, interior decorating, signature perfume making, traveling, and listening to music when not working.

Connect with Kemi:

Books Published
Love, Sex, Lies and Reality
Being Single: A State for the Fragile Heart
Beyond the Pain: A Return to Love
On Becoming Restored

Social Media
Facebook: www.facebook.com/lovesexliesandreality
Twitter: @kemisogunle
Instagram: @kemisogunle
Website: www.kemisogunle.com
Email: coaching@kemisogunle.com
YouTube: www.youtube.com/c/kemisogunle

www.ingramcontent.com/pod-product-compliance
Lightning Source LLC
Chambersburg PA
CBHW070552010526
44118CB00012B/1299